T&P BOOKS

DICTIONARY

THEME – BASED

British English Collection

ENGLISH-
INDONESIAN

The most useful words
To expand your lexicon and sharpen
your language skills

7000 words

Theme-based dictionary British English-Indonesian - 7000 words
By Andrey Taranov

T&P Books vocabularies are intended for helping you learn, memorize and review foreign words. The dictionary is divided into themes, covering all major spheres of everyday activities, business, science, culture, etc.

The process of learning words using T&P Books' theme-based dictionaries gives you the following advantages:

- Correctly grouped source information predetermines success at subsequent stages of word memorization
- Availability of words derived from the same root allowing memorization of word units (rather than separate words)
- Small units of words facilitate the process of establishing associative links needed for consolidation of vocabulary
- Level of language knowledge can be estimated by the number of learned words

T&P Books Publishing
www.tpbooks.com

This book is also available in E-book formats.
Please visit www.tpbooks.com or the major online bookstores.

INDONESIAN THEME-BASED DICTIONARY
British English collection

T&P Books vocabularies are intended to help you learn, memorize, and review foreign words. The vocabulary contains over 7000 commonly used words arranged thematically.

- Vocabulary contains the most commonly used words
- Recommended as an addition to any language course
- Meets the needs of beginners and advanced learners of foreign languages
- Convenient for daily use, revision sessions, and self-testing activities
- Allows you to assess your vocabulary

Special features of the vocabulary

- Words are organized according to their meaning, not alphabetically
- Words are presented in three columns to facilitate the reviewing and self-testing processes
- Words in groups are divided into small blocks to facilitate the learning process
- The vocabulary offers a convenient and simple transcription of each foreign word

The vocabulary has 198 topics including:

Basic Concepts, Numbers, Colors, Months, Seasons, Units of Measurement, Clothing & Accessories, Food & Nutrition, Restaurant, Family Members, Relatives, Character, Feelings, Emotions, Diseases, City, Town, Sightseeing, Shopping, Money, House, Home, Office, Working in the Office, Import & Export, Marketing, Job Search, Sports, Education, Computer, Internet, Tools, Nature, Countries, Nationalities and more ...

TABLE OF CONTENTS

PRONUNCIATION GUIDE

Letter	Indonesian example	T&P phonetic alphabet	English example
Aa	zaman	[a]	shorter than in 'ask'
Bb	besar	[b]	baby, book
Cc	kecil, cepat	[tʃ]	church, French
Dd	dugaan	[d]	day, doctor
Ee	segera, mencium	[e], [ə]	medal, elm
Ff	berfungsi	[f]	face, food
Gg	juga, lagi	[g]	game, gold
Hh	hanya, bahwa	[h]	home, have
Ii	izin, sebagai ganti	[i], [j]	Peter, yard
Jj	setuju, ijin	[dʒ]	jeans, gin
Kk	kemudian, tidak	[k], [']	kiss, glottal stop
Ll	dilarang	[l]	lace, people
Mm	melihat	[m]	magic, milk
Nn	berenang	[n], [ŋ]	name, ring
Oo	toko roti	[o:]	fall, bomb
Pp	peribahasa	[p]	pencil, private
Qq	Aquarius	[k]	clock, kiss
Rr	ratu, riang	[r]	trilled [r]
Ss	sendok, syarat	[s], [ʃ]	city, machine
Tt	tamu, adat	[t]	tourist, trip
Uu	ambulans	[u]	book
Vv	renovasi	[v]	very, river
Ww	pariwisata	[w]	vase, winter
Xx	boxer	[ks]	box, taxi
Yy	banyak, syarat	[j]	yes, New York
Zz	zamrud	[z]	zebra, please

Combinations of letters

aa	maaf	[a'a]	a+glottal stop
kh	khawatir	[h]	home, have
th	Gereja Lutheran	[t]	tourist, trip
-k	tidak	[']	glottal stop

ABBREVIATIONS
used in the dictionary

English abbreviations

ab.	-	about
adj	-	adjective
adv	-	adverb
anim.	-	animate
as adj	-	attributive noun used as adjective
e.g.	-	for example
etc.	-	et cetera
fam.	-	familiar
fem.	-	feminine
form.	-	formal
inanim.	-	inanimate
masc.	-	masculine
math	-	mathematics
mil.	-	military
n	-	noun
pl	-	plural
pron.	-	pronoun
sb	-	somebody
sing.	-	singular
sth	-	something
v aux	-	auxiliary verb
vi	-	intransitive verb
vi, vt	-	intransitive, transitive verb
vt	-	transitive verb

BASIC CONCEPTS

Basic concepts. Part 1

1. Pronouns

I, me	saya, aku	[saja], [aku]
you	engkau, kamu	[eŋkau], [kamu]
he, she, it	beliau, dia, ia	[beliau], [dia], [ia]
we	kami, kita	[kami], [kita]
you (to a group)	kalian	[kalian]
you (polite, sing.)	Anda	[anda]
you (polite, pl)	Anda sekalian	[anda sekalian]
they	mereka	[mereka]

2. Greetings. Salutations. Farewells

Hello! (fam.)	Halo!	[halo!]
Hello! (form.)	Halo!	[halo!]
Good morning!	Selamat pagi!	[slamat pagi!]
Good afternoon!	Selamat siang!	[slamat siaŋ!]
Good evening!	Selamat sore!	[slamat sore!]
to say hello	menyapa	[mənjapa]
Hi! (hello)	Hai!	[hey!]
greeting (n)	sambutan, salam	[sambutan], [salam]
to greet (vt)	menyambut	[mənjambut]
How are you?	Apa kabar?	[apa kabar?]
What's new?	Apa yang baru?	[apa yaŋ baru?]
Goodbye!	Selamat tinggal!	[slamat tiŋgal!],
	Selamat jalan!	[slamat dʒʲalan!]
Bye!	Dadah!	[dadah!]
See you soon!	Sampai bertemu lagi!	[sampaj bərtemu lagi!]
Farewell! (to a friend)	Sampai jumpa!	[sampaj dʒʲumpa!]
Farewell! (form.)	Selamat tinggal!	[slamat tiŋgal!]
to say goodbye	berpamitan	[bərpamitan]
Cheers!	Sampai nanti!	[sampaj nanti!]
Thank you! Cheers!	Terima kasih!	[tərima kasih!]
Thank you very much!	Terima kasih banyak!	[tərima kasih banjaʔ!]
My pleasure!	Kembali! Sama-sama!	[kembali!], [sama-sama!]
Don't mention it!	Kembali!	[kembali!]
It was nothing	Kembali!	[kembali!]
Excuse me!	Maaf, ...	[maʔaf, ...]
to excuse (forgive)	memaafkan	[memaʔafkan]

to apologize (vi)	meminta maaf	[meminta ma'af]
My apologies	Maafkan saya	[ma'afkan saja]
I'm sorry!	Maaf!	[ma'af!]
to forgive (vt)	memaafkan	[mema'afkan]
It's okay! (that's all right)	Tidak apa-apa!	[tida' apa-apa!]
please (adv)	tolong	[toloŋ]

Don't forget!	Jangan lupa!	[dʒ'aŋan lupa!]
Certainly!	Tentu!	[tentu!]
Of course not!	Tentu tidak!	[tentu tida'!]
Okay! (I agree)	Baiklah! Baik!	[bajklah!], [baj'!]
That's enough!	Cukuplah!	[ʧukuplah!]

3. Cardinal numbers. Part 1

0 zero	nol	[nol]
1 one	satu	[satu]
2 two	dua	[dua]
3 three	tiga	[tiga]
4 four	empat	[empat]

5 five	lima	[lima]
6 six	enam	[enam]
7 seven	tujuh	[tudʒ'uh]
8 eight	delapan	[delapan]
9 nine	sembilan	[sembilan]

10 ten	sepuluh	[sepuluh]
11 eleven	sebelas	[sebelas]
12 twelve	dua belas	[dua belas]
13 thirteen	tiga belas	[tiga belas]
14 fourteen	empat belas	[empat belas]

15 fifteen	lima belas	[lima belas]
16 sixteen	enam belas	[enam belas]
17 seventeen	tujuh belas	[tudʒ'uh belas]
18 eighteen	delapan belas	[delapan belas]
19 nineteen	sembilan belas	[sembilan belas]

20 twenty	dua puluh	[dua puluh]
21 twenty-one	dua puluh satu	[dua puluh satu]
22 twenty-two	dua puluh dua	[dua puluh dua]
23 twenty-three	dua puluh tiga	[dua puluh tiga]

30 thirty	tiga puluh	[tiga puluh]
31 thirty-one	tiga puluh satu	[tiga puluh satu]
32 thirty-two	tiga puluh dua	[tiga puluh dua]
33 thirty-three	tiga puluh tiga	[tiga puluh tiga]

40 forty	empat puluh	[empat puluh]
41 forty-one	empat puluh satu	[empat puluh satu]
42 forty-two	empat puluh dua	[empat puluh dua]
43 forty-three	empat puluh tiga	[empat puluh tiga]
50 fifty	lima puluh	[lima puluh]

51 fifty-one	lima puluh satu	[lima puluh satu]
52 fifty-two	lima puluh dua	[lima puluh dua]
53 fifty-three	lima puluh tiga	[lima puluh tiga]
60 sixty	enam puluh	[enam puluh]
61 sixty-one	enam puluh satu	[enam puluh satu]
62 sixty-two	enam puluh dua	[enam puluh dua]
63 sixty-three	enam puluh tiga	[enam puluh tiga]
70 seventy	tujuh puluh	[tudʒuh puluh]
71 seventy-one	tujuh puluh satu	[tudʒuh puluh satu]
72 seventy-two	tujuh puluh dua	[tudʒuh puluh dua]
73 seventy-three	tujuh puluh tiga	[tudʒuh puluh tiga]
80 eighty	delapan puluh	[delapan puluh]
81 eighty-one	delapan puluh satu	[delapan puluh satu]
82 eighty-two	delapan puluh dua	[delapan puluh dua]
83 eighty-three	delapan puluh tiga	[delapan puluh tiga]
90 ninety	sembilan puluh	[sembilan puluh]
91 ninety-one	sembulan puluh satu	[sembulan puluh satu]
92 ninety-two	sembilan puluh dua	[sembilan puluh dua]
93 ninety-three	sembilan puluh tiga	[sembilan puluh tiga]

4. Cardinal numbers. Part 2

100 one hundred	seratus	[seratus]
200 two hundred	dua ratus	[dua ratus]
300 three hundred	tiga ratus	[tiga ratus]
400 four hundred	empat ratus	[empat ratus]
500 five hundred	lima ratus	[lima ratus]
600 six hundred	enam ratus	[enam ratus]
700 seven hundred	tujuh ratus	[tudʒuh ratus]
800 eight hundred	delapan ratus	[delapan ratus]
900 nine hundred	sembilan ratus	[sembilan ratus]
1000 one thousand	seribu	[seribu]
2000 two thousand	dua ribu	[dua ribu]
3000 three thousand	tiga ribu	[tiga ribu]
10000 ten thousand	sepuluh ribu	[sepuluh ribu]
one hundred thousand	seratus ribu	[seratus ribu]
million	juta	[dʒuta]
billion	miliar	[miliar]

5. Numbers. Fractions

fraction	pecahan	[petʃahan]
one half	seperdua	[seperdua]
one third	sepertiga	[sepertiga]
one quarter	seperempat	[seperempat]
one eighth	seperdelapan	[seperdelapan]

one tenth	sepersepuluh	[sepersepuluh]
two thirds	dua pertiga	[dua pərtiga]
three quarters	tiga perempat	[tiga pərempat]

6. Numbers. Basic operations

subtraction	pengurangan	[pəŋuraŋan]
to subtract (vi, vt)	mengurangkan	[məŋuraŋkan]
division	pembagian	[pembagian]
to divide (vt)	membagi	[membagi]

addition	penambahan	[penambahan]
to add up (vt)	menambahkan	[mənambahkan]
to add (vi)	menambahkan	[mənambahkan]
multiplication	pengalian	[peŋalian]
to multiply (vt)	mengalikan	[məŋalikan]

7. Numbers. Miscellaneous

digit, figure	angka	[aŋka]
number	nomor	[nomor]
numeral	kata bilangan	[kata bilaŋan]
minus sign	minus	[minus]
plus sign	plus	[plus]
formula	rumus	[rumus]

calculation	perhitungan	[pərhituŋan]
to count (vi, vt)	menghitung	[məŋhituŋ]
to count up	menghitung	[məŋhituŋ]
to compare (vt)	membandingkan	[membandiŋkan]

How much?	Berapa?	[bərapa?]
sum, total	jumlah	[dʒʲumlah]
result	hasil	[hasil]
remainder	sisa, baki	[sisa], [baki]
a few (e.g., ~ years ago)	beberapa	[beberapa]
little (I had ~ time)	sedikit	[sedikit]
the rest	selebihnya, sisanya	[selebihnja], [sisanja]
one and a half	satu setengah	[satu seteŋah]
dozen	lusin	[lusin]

in half (adv)	dua bagian	[dua bagian]
equally (evenly)	rata	[rata]
half	setengah	[seteŋah]
time (three ~s)	kali	[kali]

8. The most important verbs. Part 1

| to advise (vt) | menasihati | [mənasihati] |
| to agree (say yes) | setuju | [setudʒʲu] |

to answer (vi, vt)	**menjawab**	[mənʤawab]
to apologize (vi)	**meminta maaf**	[meminta ma'af]
to arrive (vi)	**datang**	[dataŋ]

to ask (~ oneself)	**bertanya**	[bərtanja]
to ask (~ sb to do sth)	**meminta**	[meminta]
to be (~ a teacher)	**ialah, adalah**	[ialah], [adalah]
to be (~ on a diet)	**sedang**	[sedaŋ]

to be afraid	**takut**	[takut]
to be hungry	**lapar**	[lapar]
to be interested in …	**menaruh minat pada …**	[mənaruh minat pada …]
to be needed	**dibutuhkan**	[dibutuhkan]
to be surprised	**heran**	[heran]

to be thirsty	**haus**	[haus]
to begin (vt)	**memulai, membuka**	[memulaj], [membuka]
to belong to …	**kepunyaan …**	[kepunja'an …]
to boast (vi)	**membual**	[membual]
to break (split into pieces)	**memecahkan**	[memetʃahkan]
to call (~ for help)	**memanggil**	[memaŋgil]

can (v aux)	**bisa**	[bisa]
to catch (vt)	**menangkap**	[mənaŋkap]
to change (vt)	**mengubah**	[məŋubah]
to choose (select)	**memilih**	[memilih]
to come down (the stairs)	**turun**	[turun]

to compare (vt)	**membandingkan**	[membandiŋkan]
to complain (vi, vt)	**mengeluh**	[məŋeluh]
to confuse (mix up)	**bingung membedakan**	[biŋuŋ membedakan]
to continue (vt)	**meneruskan**	[məneruskan]
to control (vt)	**mengontrol**	[məŋontrol]
to cook (dinner)	**memasak**	[memasa']

to cost (vt)	**berharga**	[bərharga]
to count (add up)	**menghitung**	[məŋhituŋ]
to count on …	**mengharapkan …**	[məŋharapkan …]
to create (vt)	**menciptakan**	[məntʃiptakan]
to cry (weep)	**menangis**	[mənaŋis]

9. The most important verbs. Part 2

to deceive (vi, vt)	**menipu**	[mənipu]
to decorate (tree, street)	**menghiasi**	[məŋhiasi]
to defend (a country, etc.)	**membela**	[membela]
to demand (request firmly)	**menuntut**	[mənuntut]
to dig (vt)	**menggali**	[məŋgali]

to discuss (vt)	**membicarakan**	[membitʃarakan]
to do (vt)	**membuat**	[membuat]
to doubt (have doubts)	**ragu-ragu**	[ragu-ragu]
to drop (let fall)	**tercecer**	[tərtʃetʃer]
to enter (room, house, etc.)	**masuk, memasuki**	[masuk], [memasuki]

to excuse (forgive)	memaafkan	[mema'afkan]
to exist (vi)	ada	[ada]
to expect (foresee)	menduga	[mənduga]
to explain (vt)	menjelaskan	[məndʒˈelaskan]
to fall (vi)	jatuh	[dʒˈatuh]
to fancy (vt)	suka	[suka]
to find (vt)	menemukan	[mənemukan]
to finish (vt)	mengakhiri	[məŋahiri]
to fly (vi)	terbang	[tərbaŋ]
to follow ... (come after)	mengikuti ...	[məŋikuti ...]
to forget (vi, vt)	melupakan	[melupakan]
to forgive (vt)	memaafkan	[mema'afkan]
to give (vt)	memberi	[memberi]
to give a hint	memberi petunjuk	[memberi petundʒˈu']
to go (on foot)	berjalan	[bərdʒˈalan]
to go for a swim	berenang	[bərenaŋ]
to go out (for dinner, etc.)	keluar	[keluar]
to guess (the answer)	menerka	[mənerka]
to have (vt)	mempunyai	[mempunjaj]
to have breakfast	sarapan	[sarapan]
to have dinner	makan malam	[makan malam]
to have lunch	makan siang	[makan siaŋ]
to hear (vt)	mendengar	[məndeŋar]
to help (vt)	membantu	[membantu]
to hide (vt)	menyembunyikan	[mənjembunjikan]
to hope (vi, vt)	berharap	[bərharap]
to hunt (vi, vt)	berburu	[bərburu]
to hurry (vi)	tergesa-gesa	[tərgesa-gesa]

10. The most important verbs. Part 3

to inform (vt)	menginformasikan	[məŋinformasikan]
to insist (vi, vt)	mendesak	[məndesa']
to insult (vt)	menghina	[məŋhina]
to invite (vt)	mengundang	[məŋundaŋ]
to joke (vi)	bergurau	[bərgurau]
to keep (vt)	menyimpan	[mənjimpan]
to keep silent, to hush	diam	[diam]
to kill (vt)	membunuh	[membunuh]
to know (sb)	kenal	[kenal]
to know (sth)	tahu	[tahu]
to laugh (vi)	tertawa	[tərtawa]
to liberate (city, etc.)	membebaskan	[membebaskan]
to look for ... (search)	mencari ...	[məntʃari ...]
to love (sb)	mencintai	[məntʃintaj]
to make a mistake	salah	[salah]
to manage, to run	memimpin	[memimpin]

to mean (signify)	**berarti**	[bərarti]
to mention (talk about)	**menyebut**	[mənjebut]
to miss (school, etc.)	**absen**	[absen]
to notice (see)	**memperhatikan**	[memperhatikan]
to object (vi, vt)	**keberatan**	[keberatan]
to observe (see)	**mengamati**	[məŋamati]
to open (vt)	**membuka**	[membuka]
to order (meal, etc.)	**memesan**	[memesan]
to order (mil.)	**memerintahkan**	[memerintahkan]
to own (possess)	**memiliki**	[memiliki]
to participate (vi)	**turut serta**	[turut serta]
to pay (vi, vt)	**membayar**	[membajar]
to permit (vt)	**mengizinkan**	[məŋizinkan]
to plan (vt)	**merencanakan**	[merentʃanakan]
to play (children)	**bermain**	[bərmajn]
to pray (vi, vt)	**bersembahyang, berdoa**	[bərsembahjaŋ], [bərdoa]
to prefer (vt)	**lebih suka**	[lebih suka]
to promise (vt)	**berjanji**	[bərdʒˈandʒi]
to pronounce (vt)	**melafalkan**	[melafalkan]
to propose (vt)	**mengusulkan**	[məŋusulkan]
to punish (vt)	**menghukum**	[məŋhukum]

11. The most important verbs. Part 4

to read (vi, vt)	**membaca**	[membatʃa]
to recommend (vt)	**merekomendasi**	[merekomendasi]
to refuse (vi, vt)	**menolak**	[mənolaʔ]
to regret (be sorry)	**menyesal**	[mənjesal]
to rent (sth from sb)	**menyewa**	[mənjewa]
to repeat (say again)	**mengulangi**	[məŋulaŋi]
to reserve, to book	**memesan**	[memesan]
to run (vi)	**lari**	[lari]
to save (rescue)	**menyelamatkan**	[mənjelamatkan]
to say (~ thank you)	**berkata**	[bərkata]
to scold (vt)	**memarahi, menegur**	[memarahi], [menegur]
to see (vt)	**melihat**	[melihat]
to sell (vt)	**menjual**	[məndʒˈual]
to send (vt)	**mengirim**	[məŋirim]
to shoot (vi)	**menembak**	[mənembaʔ]
to shout (vi)	**berteriak**	[bərteriaʔ]
to show (vt)	**menunjukkan**	[mənundʒˈuʔkan]
to sign (document)	**menandatangani**	[mənandataŋani]
to sit down (vi)	**duduk**	[duduʔ]
to smile (vi)	**tersenyum**	[tərsenyum]
to speak (vi, vt)	**berbicara**	[bərbitʃara]
to steal (money, etc.)	**mencuri**	[məntʃuri]
to stop (for pause, etc.)	**berhenti**	[bərhenti]

to stop (please ~ calling me)	menghentikan	[məŋhentikan]
to study (vt)	mempelajari	[mempeladʒiari]
to swim (vi)	berenang	[bərenaŋ]
to take (vt)	mengambil	[məŋambil]
to think (vi, vt)	berpikir	[bərpikir]

to threaten (vt)	mengancam	[məŋantʃam]
to touch (with hands)	menyentuh	[mənjentuh]
to translate (vt)	menerjemahkan	[mənerdʒiemahkan]
to trust (vt)	mempercayai	[mempertʃajaj]
to try (attempt)	mencoba	[məntʃoba]

to turn (e.g., ~ left)	membelok	[membeloʔ]
to underestimate (vt)	meremehkan	[meremehkan]
to understand (vt)	mengerti	[məŋerti]
to unite (vt)	menyatukan	[mənjatukan]
to wait (vt)	menunggu	[mənuŋgu]

to want (wish, desire)	mau, ingin	[mau], [iŋin]
to warn (vt)	memperingatkan	[memperiŋatkan]
to work (vi)	bekerja	[bekerdʒia]
to write (vt)	menulis	[mənulis]
to write down	mencatat	[məntʃatat]

12. Colours

colour	warna	[warna]
shade (tint)	nuansa	[nuansa]
hue	warna	[warna]
rainbow	pelangi	[pelaŋi]

white (adj)	putih	[putih]
black (adj)	hitam	[hitam]
grey (adj)	kelabu	[kelabu]

green (adj)	hijau	[hidʒiau]
yellow (adj)	kuning	[kuniŋ]
red (adj)	merah	[merah]

blue (adj)	biru	[biru]
light blue (adj)	biru muda	[biru muda]
pink (adj)	pink	[pinʔ]
orange (adj)	oranye, jingga	[oranje], [dʒiŋga]
violet (adj)	violet, ungu muda	[violet], [uŋu muda]
brown (adj)	cokelat	[tʃokelat]

| golden (adj) | keemasan | [keemasan] |
| silvery (adj) | keperakan | [keperakan] |

beige (adj)	abu-abu kecokelatan	[abu-abu ketʃokelatan]
cream (adj)	krem	[krem]
turquoise (adj)	pirus	[pirus]
cherry red (adj)	merah tua	[merah tua]
lilac (adj)	ungu	[uŋu]

crimson (adj)	merah lembayung	[merah lembajuŋ]
light (adj)	terang	[teraŋ]
dark (adj)	gelap	[gelap]
bright, vivid (adj)	terang	[teraŋ]

coloured (pencils)	berwarna	[bərwarna]
colour (e.g. ~ film)	warna	[warna]
black-and-white (adj)	hitam-putih	[hitam-putih]
plain (one-coloured)	polos, satu warna	[polos], [satu warna]
multicoloured (adj)	berwarna-warni	[bərwarna-warni]

13. Questions

Who?	Siapa?	[siapa?]
What?	Apa?	[apa?]
Where? (at, in)	Di mana?	[di mana?]
Where (to)?	Ke mana?	[ke mana?]
From where?	Dari mana?	[dari mana?]
When?	Kapan?	[kapan?]
Why? (What for?)	Mengapa?	[mənapa?]
Why? (~ are you crying?)	Mengapa?	[mənapa?]

What for?	Untuk apa?	[untu' apa?]
How? (in what way)	Bagaimana?	[bagajmana?]
What? (What kind of ...?)	Apa? Yang mana?	[apa?], [yaŋ mana?]
Which?	Yang mana?	[yaŋ mana?]

To whom?	Kepada siapa? Untuk siapa?	[kepada siapa?], [untu' siapa?]
About whom?	Tentang siapa?	[tentaŋ siapa?]
About what?	Tentang apa?	[tentaŋ apa?]
With whom?	Dengan siapa?	[deŋan siapa?]

How many? How much?	Berapa?	[bərapa?]
Whose?	Milik siapa?	[mili' siapa?]

14. Function words. Adverbs. Part 1

Where? (at, in)	Di mana?	[di mana?]
here (adv)	di sini	[di sini]
there (adv)	di sana	[di sana]

somewhere (to be)	di suatu tempat	[di suatu tempat]
nowhere (not in any place)	tak ada di mana pun	[ta' ada di mana pun]

by (near, beside)	dekat	[dekat]
by the window	dekat jendela	[dekat dʒ'endela]

Where (to)?	Ke mana?	[ke mana?]
here (e.g. come ~!)	ke sini	[ke sini]
there (e.g. to go ~)	ke sana	[ke sana]
from here (adv)	dari sini	[dari sini]

from there (adv)	dari sana	[dari sana]
close (adv)	dekat	[dekat]
far (adv)	jauh	[dʒ'auh]

near (e.g. ~ Paris)	dekat	[dekat]
nearby (adv)	dekat	[dekat]
not far (adv)	tidak jauh	[tida' dʒ'auh]

left (adj)	kiri	[kiri]
on the left	di kiri	[di kiri]
to the left	ke kiri	[ke kiri]

right (adj)	kanan	[kanan]
on the right	di kanan	[di kanan]
to the right	ke kanan	[ke kanan]

in front (adv)	di depan	[di depan]
front (as adj)	depan	[depan]
ahead (the kids ran ~)	ke depan	[ke depan]

behind (adv)	di belakang	[di belakaŋ]
from behind	dari belakang	[dari belakaŋ]
back (towards the rear)	mundur	[mundur]

| middle | tengah | [teŋah] |
| in the middle | di tengah | [di teŋah] |

at the side	di sisi, di samping	[di sisi], [di sampiŋ]
everywhere (adv)	di mana-mana	[di mana-mana]
around (in all directions)	di sekitar	[di sekitar]

from inside	dari dalam	[dari dalam]
somewhere (to go)	ke suatu tempat	[ke suatu tempat]
straight (directly)	terus	[terus]
back (e.g. come ~)	kembali	[kembali]

| from anywhere | dari mana pun | [dari mana pun] |
| from somewhere | dari suatu tempat | [dari suatu tempat] |

firstly (adv)	pertama	[pertama]
secondly (adv)	kedua	[kedua]
thirdly (adv)	ketiga	[ketiga]

suddenly (adv)	tiba-tiba	[tiba-tiba]
at first (in the beginning)	mula-mula	[mula-mula]
for the first time	untuk pertama kalinya	[untu' pertama kalinja]
long before …	jauh sebelum …	[dʒ'auh sebelum …]
anew (over again)	kembali	[kembali]
for good (adv)	untuk selama-lamanya	[untu' selama-lamanja]

never (adv)	tidak pernah	[tida' pernah]
again (adv)	lagi, kembali	[lagi], [kembali]
now (at present)	sekarang	[sekaraŋ]
often (adv)	sering, seringkali	[seriŋ], [seriŋkali]
then (adv)	ketika itu	[ketika itu]
urgently (quickly)	segera	[segera]

usually (adv)	biasanya	[biasanja]
by the way, ...	ngomong-ngomong ...	[ŋomoŋ-ŋomoŋ ...]
possibly	mungkin	[muŋkin]
probably (adv)	mungkin	[muŋkin]
maybe (adv)	mungkin	[muŋkin]
besides ...	selain itu ...	[selajn itu ...]
that's why ...	karena itu ...	[karena itu ...]
in spite of ...	meskipun ...	[meskipun ...]
thanks to ...	berkat ...	[berkat ...]

what (pron.)	apa	[apa]
that (conj.)	bahwa	[bahwa]
something	sesuatu	[sesuatu]
anything (something)	sesuatu	[sesuatu]
nothing	tidak sesuatu pun	[tida' sesuatu pun]

who (pron.)	siapa	[siapa]
someone	seseorang	[seseoraŋ]
somebody	seseorang	[seseoraŋ]

nobody	tidak seorang pun	[tida' seoraŋ pun]
nowhere (a voyage to ~)	tidak ke mana pun	[tida' ke mana pun]
nobody's	tidak milik siapa pun	[tida' mili' siapa pun]
somebody's	milik seseorang	[mili' seseoraŋ]

so (I'm ~ glad)	sangat	[saŋat]
also (as well)	juga	[ʤ'uga]
too (as well)	juga	[ʤ'uga]

15. Function words. Adverbs. Part 2

Why?	Mengapa?	[məŋapa?]
for some reason	entah mengapa	[entah məŋapa]
because ...	karena ...	[karena ...]
for some purpose	untuk tujuan tertentu	[untu' tuʤ'uan tərtentu]

and	dan	[dan]
or	atau	[atau]
but	tetapi, namun	[tetapi], [namun]
for (e.g. ~ me)	untuk	[untu']

too (excessively)	terlalu	[tərlalu]
only (exclusively)	hanya	[hanja]
exactly (adv)	tepat	[tepat]
about (more or less)	sekitar	[sekitar]

approximately (adv)	kira-kira	[kira-kira]
approximate (adj)	kira-kira	[kira-kira]
almost (adv)	hampir	[hampir]
the rest	selebihnya, sisanya	[selebihnja], [sisanja]

the other (second)	kedua	[kedua]
other (different)	lain	[lain]
each (adj)	setiap	[setiap]

any (no matter which)	sebarang	[sebaraŋ]
many, much (a lot of)	banyak	[banjaʔ]
many people	banyak orang	[banjaʔ oraŋ]
all (everyone)	semua	[semua]

in return for …	sebagai ganti …	[sebagaj ganti …]
in exchange (adv)	sebagai gantinya	[sebagaj gantinja]
by hand (made)	dengan tangan	[deŋan taŋan]
hardly (negative opinion)	hampir tidak	[hampir tidaʔ]

probably (adv)	mungkin	[muŋkin]
on purpose (intentionally)	sengaja	[seŋadʒʲa]
by accident (adv)	tidak sengaja	[tidaʔ seŋadʒʲa]

very (adv)	sangat	[saŋat]
for example (adv)	misalnya	[misalnja]
between	antara	[antara]
among	di antara	[di antara]
so much (such a lot)	banyak sekali	[banjaʔ sekali]
especially (adv)	terutama	[terutama]

Basic concepts. Part 2

16. Opposites

rich (adj)	**kaya**	[kaja]
poor (adj)	**miskin**	[miskin]
ill, sick (adj)	**sakit**	[sakit]
well (not sick)	**sehat**	[sehat]
big (adj)	**besar**	[besar]
small (adj)	**kecil**	[ketʃil]
quickly (adv)	**cepat**	[tʃepat]
slowly (adv)	**perlahan-lahan**	[pərlahan-lahan]
fast (adj)	**cepat**	[tʃepat]
slow (adj)	**lambat**	[lambat]
glad (adj)	**riang**	[riaŋ]
sad (adj)	**sedih**	[sedih]
together (adv)	**bersama**	[bərsama]
separately (adv)	**terpisah**	[tərpisah]
aloud (to read)	**dengan keras**	[deŋan keras]
silently (to oneself)	**dalam hati**	[dalam hati]
tall (adj)	**tinggi**	[tiŋgi]
low (adj)	**rendah**	[rendah]
deep (adj)	**dalam**	[dalam]
shallow (adj)	**dangkal**	[daŋkal]
yes	**ya**	[ya]
no	**tidak**	[tidaʔ]
distant (in space)	**jauh**	[dʒʲauh]
nearby (adj)	**dekat**	[dekat]
far (adv)	**jauh**	[dʒʲauh]
nearby (adv)	**dekat**	[dekat]
long (adj)	**panjang**	[pandʒʲaŋ]
short (adj)	**pendek**	[pendeʔ]
good (kindhearted)	**baik hati**	[bajʔ hati]
evil (adj)	**jahat**	[dʒʲahat]

married (adj)	menikah	[mənikah]
single (adj)	bujang	[budʒˈaŋ]
to forbid (vt)	melarang	[melaraŋ]
to permit (vt)	mengizinkan	[məŋizinkan]
end	akhir	[ahir]
beginning	permulaan	[pərmulaʔan]
left (adj)	kiri	[kiri]
right (adj)	kanan	[kanan]
first (adj)	pertama	[pərtama]
last (adj)	terakhir	[tərahir]
crime	kejahatan	[kedʒˈahatan]
punishment	hukuman	[hukuman]
to order (vt)	memerintahkan	[memerintahkan]
to obey (vi, vt)	mematuhi	[mematuhi]
straight (adj)	lurus	[lurus]
curved (adj)	melengkung	[meleŋkuŋ]
paradise	surga	[surga]
hell	neraka	[neraka]
to be born	lahir	[lahir]
to die (vi)	mati, meninggal	[mati], [meniŋgal]
strong (adj)	kuat	[kuat]
weak (adj)	lemah	[lemah]
old (adj)	tua	[tua]
young (adj)	muda	[muda]
old (adj)	tua	[tua]
new (adj)	baru	[baru]
hard (adj)	keras	[keras]
soft (adj)	lunak	[lunaʔ]
warm (tepid)	hangat	[haŋat]
cold (adj)	dingin	[diŋin]
fat (adj)	gemuk	[gemuʔ]
thin (adj)	kurus	[kurus]
narrow (adj)	sempit	[sempit]
wide (adj)	lebar	[lebar]
good (adj)	baik	[bajʔ]
bad (adj)	buruk	[buruʔ]
brave (adj)	pemberani	[pemberani]
cowardly (adj)	penakut	[penakut]

17. Weekdays

Monday	**Hari Senin**	[hari senin]
Tuesday	**Hari Selasa**	[hari selasa]
Wednesday	**Hari Rabu**	[hari rabu]
Thursday	**Hari Kamis**	[hari kamis]
Friday	**Hari Jumat**	[hari dʒʲumat]
Saturday	**Hari Sabtu**	[hari sabtu]
Sunday	**Hari Minggu**	[hari miŋgu]
today (adv)	**hari ini**	[hari ini]
tomorrow (adv)	**besok**	[besoʔ]
the day after tomorrow	**besok lusa**	[besoʔ lusa]
yesterday (adv)	**kemarin**	[kemarin]
the day before yesterday	**kemarin dulu**	[kemarin dulu]
day	**hari**	[hari]
working day	**hari kerja**	[hari kerdʒʲa]
public holiday	**hari libur**	[hari libur]
day off	**hari libur**	[hari libur]
weekend	**akhir pekan**	[ahir pekan]
all day long	**seharian**	[seharian]
the next day (adv)	**hari berikutnya**	[hari bərikutnja]
two days ago	**dua hari lalu**	[dua hari lalu]
the day before	**hari sebelumnya**	[hari sebelumnja]
daily (adj)	**harian**	[harian]
every day (adv)	**tiap hari**	[tiap hari]
week	**minggu**	[miŋgu]
last week (adv)	**minggu lalu**	[miŋgu lalu]
next week (adv)	**minggu berikutnya**	[miŋu bərikutnja]
weekly (adj)	**mingguan**	[miŋguan]
every week (adv)	**tiap minggu**	[tiap miŋgu]
twice a week	**dua kali seminggu**	[dua kali semiŋgu]
every Tuesday	**tiap Hari Selasa**	[tiap hari selasa]

18. Hours. Day and night

morning	**pagi**	[pagi]
in the morning	**pada pagi hari**	[pada pagi hari]
noon, midday	**tengah hari**	[teŋah hari]
in the afternoon	**pada sore hari**	[pada sore hari]
evening	**sore, malam**	[sore], [malam]
in the evening	**waktu sore**	[waktu sore]
night	**malam**	[malam]
at night	**pada malam hari**	[pada malam hari]
midnight	**tengah malam**	[teŋah malam]
second	**detik**	[detiʔ]
minute	**menit**	[menit]
hour	**jam**	[dʒʲam]

half an hour	setengah jam	[setengah dʒiam]
a quarter-hour	seperempat jam	[seperempat dʒiam]
fifteen minutes	lima belas menit	[lima belas menit]
24 hours	siang-malam	[siaŋ-malam]

sunrise	matahari terbit	[matahari tərbit]
dawn	subuh	[subuh]
early morning	dini pagi	[dini pagi]
sunset	matahari terbenam	[matahari tərbenam]

early in the morning	pagi-pagi	[pagi-pagi]
this morning	pagi ini	[pagi ini]
tomorrow morning	besok pagi	[beso' pagi]

this afternoon	sore ini	[sore ini]
in the afternoon	pada sore hari	[pada sore hari]
tomorrow afternoon	besok sore	[beso' sore]

| tonight (this evening) | sore ini | [sore ini] |
| tomorrow night | besok malam | [beso' malam] |

at 3 o'clock sharp	pukul 3 tepat	[pukul tiga tepat]
about 4 o'clock	sekitar pukul 4	[sekitar pukul empat]
by 12 o'clock	pada pukul 12	[pada pukul belas]

in 20 minutes	dalam 20 menit	[dalam dua puluh menit]
in an hour	dalam satu jam	[dalam satu dʒiam]
on time (adv)	tepat waktu	[tepat waktu]

a quarter to …	… kurang seperempat	[… kuraŋ seperempat]
within an hour	selama sejam	[selama sedʒiam]
every 15 minutes	tiap 15 menit	[tiap lima belas menit]
round the clock	siang-malam	[siaŋ-malam]

19. Months. Seasons

January	Januari	[dʒianuari]
February	Februari	[februari]
March	Maret	[maret]
April	April	[april]
May	Mei	[mei]
June	Juni	[dʒiuni]

July	Juli	[dʒiuli]
August	Augustus	[augustus]
September	September	[september]
October	Oktober	[oktober]
November	November	[november]
December	Desember	[desember]

spring	musim semi	[musim semi]
in spring	pada musim semi	[pada musim semi]
spring (as adj)	musim semi	[musim semi]
summer	musim panas	[musim panas]

in summer	**pada musim panas**	[pada musim panas]
summer (as adj)	**musim panas**	[musim panas]
autumn	**musim gugur**	[musim gugur]
in autumn	**pada musim gugur**	[pada musim gugur]
autumn (as adj)	**musim gugur**	[musim gugur]
winter	**musim dingin**	[musim diŋin]
in winter	**pada musim dingin**	[pada musim diŋin]
winter (as adj)	**musim dingin**	[musim diŋin]
month	**bulan**	[bulan]
this month	**bulan ini**	[bulan ini]
next month	**bulan depan**	[bulan depan]
last month	**bulan lalu**	[bulan lalu]
a month ago	**sebulan lalu**	[sebulan lalu]
in a month (a month later)	**dalam satu bulan**	[dalam satu bulan]
in 2 months (2 months later)	**dalam 2 bulan**	[dalam dua bulan]
the whole month	**sepanjang bulan**	[sepandʒˈaŋ bulan]
all month long	**sebulan penuh**	[sebulan penuh]
monthly (~ magazine)	**bulanan**	[bulanan]
monthly (adv)	**tiap bulan**	[tiap bulan]
every month	**tiap bulan**	[tiap bulan]
twice a month	**dua kali sebulan**	[dua kali sebulan]
year	**tahun**	[tahun]
this year	**tahun ini**	[tahun ini]
next year	**tahun depan**	[tahun depan]
last year	**tahun lalu**	[tahun lalu]
a year ago	**setahun lalu**	[setahun lalu]
in a year	**dalam satu tahun**	[dalam satu tahun]
in two years	**dalam 2 tahun**	[dalam dua tahun]
the whole year	**sepanjang tahun**	[sepandʒˈaŋ tahun]
all year long	**setahun penuh**	[setahun penuh]
every year	**tiap tahun**	[tiap tahun]
annual (adj)	**tahunan**	[tahunan]
annually (adv)	**tiap tahun**	[tiap tahun]
4 times a year	**empat kali setahun**	[empat kali setahun]
date (e.g. today's ~)	**tanggal**	[taŋgal]
date (e.g. ~ of birth)	**tanggal**	[taŋgal]
calendar	**kalender**	[kalender]
half a year	**setengah tahun**	[seteŋah tahun]
six months	**enam bulan**	[enam bulan]
season (summer, etc.)	**musim**	[musim]
century	**abad**	[abad]

20. Time. Miscellaneous

time	**waktu**	[waktu]
moment	**sekejap**	[sekedʒˈap]

instant (n)	saat, waktu	[sa'at], [waktu]
instant (adj)	seketika	[seketika]
lapse (of time)	jangka waktu	[dʒ'aŋka waktu]
life	kehidupan, hidup	[kehidupan], [hidup]
eternity	keabadiaan	[keabadia'an]
epoch	zaman	[zaman]
era	era	[era]
cycle	siklus	[siklus]
period	periode, kurun waktu	[periode], [kurun waktu]
term (short-~)	jangka waktu	[dʒ'aŋka waktu]
the future	masa depan	[masa depan]
future (as adj)	yang akan datang	[yaŋ akan dataŋ]
next time	lain kali	[lain kali]
the past	masa lalu	[masa lalu]
past (recent)	lalu	[lalu]
last time	terakhir kali	[terahir kali]
later (adv)	kemudian	[kemudian]
after (prep.)	sesudah	[sesudah]
nowadays (adv)	sekarang	[sekaraŋ]
now (at this moment)	saat ini	[sa'at ini]
immediately (adv)	segera	[segera]
soon (adv)	segera	[segera]
in advance (beforehand)	sebelumnya	[sebelumnja]
a long time ago	dahulu kala	[dahulu kala]
recently (adv)	baru-baru ini	[baru-baru ini]
destiny	nasib	[nasib]
recollections	kenang-kenangan	[kenaŋ-kenaŋan]
archives	arsip	[arsip]
during …	selama …	[selama …]
long, a long time (adv)	lama	[lama]
not long (adv)	tidak lama	[tida' lama]
early (in the morning)	pagi-pagi	[pagi-pagi]
late (not early)	terlambat	[terlambat]
forever (for good)	untuk selama-lamanya	[untu' selama-lamanja]
to start (begin)	memulai	[memulaj]
to postpone (vt)	menunda	[menunda]
at the same time	serentak	[serenta']
permanently (adv)	tetap	[tetap]
constant (noise, pain)	terus menerus	[terus menerus]
temporary (adj)	sementara	[sementara]
sometimes (adv)	kadang-kadang	[kadaŋ-kadaŋ]
rarely (adv)	jarang	[dʒaraŋ]
often (adv)	sering, seringkali	[seriŋ], [seriŋkali]

21. Lines and shapes

square	bujur sangkar	[budʒ'ur saŋkar]
square (as adj)	persegi	[persegi]

circle	**lingkaran**	[liŋkaran]
round (adj)	**bundar**	[bundar]
triangle	**segi tiga**	[segi tiga]
triangular (adj)	**segi tiga**	[segi tiga]
oval	**oval**	[oval]
oval (as adj)	**oval**	[oval]
rectangle	**segi empat**	[segi empat]
rectangular (adj)	**siku-siku**	[siku-siku]
pyramid	**piramida**	[piramida]
rhombus	**rombus**	[rombus]
trapezium	**trapesium**	[trapesium]
cube	**kubus**	[kubus]
prism	**prisma**	[prisma]
circumference	**lingkar**	[liŋkar]
sphere	**bulatan**	[bulatan]
ball (solid sphere)	**bola**	[bola]
diameter	**diameter**	[diameter]
radius	**radius, jari-jari**	[radius], [dʒʲari-dʒʲari]
perimeter (circle's ~)	**perimeter**	[perimeter]
centre	**pusat**	[pusat]
horizontal (adj)	**horizontal, mendatar**	[horizontal], [mendatar]
vertical (adj)	**vertikal, tegak lurus**	[vertikal], [tegaʔ lurus]
parallel (n)	**sejajar**	[sedʒʲadʒʲar]
parallel (as adj)	**sejajar**	[sedʒʲadʒʲar]
line	**garis**	[garis]
stroke	**garis**	[garis]
straight line	**garis lurus**	[garis lurus]
curve (curved line)	**garis lengkung**	[garis leŋkuŋ]
thin (line, etc.)	**tipis**	[tipis]
contour (outline)	**kontur**	[kontur]
intersection	**titik potong**	[titiʔ potoŋ]
right angle	**sudut siku-siku**	[sudut siku-siku]
segment	**segmen**	[segmen]
sector (circular ~)	**sektor**	[sektor]
side (of a triangle)	**segi**	[segi]
angle	**sudut**	[sudut]

22. Units of measurement

weight	**berat**	[berat]
length	**panjang**	[pandʒʲaŋ]
width	**lebar**	[lebar]
height	**ketinggian**	[ketiŋgian]
depth	**kedalaman**	[kedalaman]
volume	**volume, isi**	[volume], [isi]
area	**luas**	[luas]
gram	**gram**	[gram]
milligram	**miligram**	[miligram]

kilogram	kilogram	[kilogram]
ton	ton	[ton]
pound	pon	[pon]
ounce	ons	[ons]

metre	meter	[meter]
millimetre	milimeter	[milimeter]
centimetre	sentimeter	[sentimeter]
kilometre	kilometer	[kilometer]
mile	mil	[mil]

inch	inci	[intʃi]
foot	kaki	[kaki]
yard	yard	[yard]

| square metre | meter persegi | [meter pərsegi] |
| hectare | hektar | [hektar] |

litre	liter	[liter]
degree	derajat	[deradʒ'at]
volt	volt	[volt]
ampere	ampere	[ampere]
horsepower	tenaga kuda	[tenaga kuda]

quantity	kuantitas	[kuantitas]
a little bit of ...	sedikit ...	[sedikit ...]
half	setengah	[seteŋah]
dozen	lusin	[lusin]
piece (item)	buah	[buah]

| size | ukuran | [ukuran] |
| scale (map ~) | skala | [skala] |

minimal (adj)	minimal	[minimal]
the smallest (adj)	terkecil	[tərketʃil]
medium (adj)	sedang	[sedaŋ]
maximal (adj)	maksimal	[maksimal]
the largest (adj)	terbesar	[tərbesar]

23. Containers

canning jar (glass ~)	gelas	[gelas]
tin, can	kaleng	[kaleŋ]
bucket	ember	[ember]
barrel	tong	[toŋ]

wash basin (e.g., plastic ~)	baskom	[baskom]
tank (100L water ~)	tangki	[taŋki]
hip flask	pelples	[pelples]
jerrycan	jeriken	[dʒ'eriken]
tank (e.g., tank car)	tangki	[taŋki]

| mug | mangkuk | [maŋkuʔ] |
| cup (of coffee, etc.) | cangkir | [tʃaŋkir] |

saucer	**alas cangkir**	[alas tʃaŋkir]
glass (tumbler)	**gelas**	[gelas]
wine glass	**gelas anggur**	[gelas aŋgur]
stock pot (soup pot)	**panci**	[pantʃi]

bottle (~ of wine)	**botol**	[botol]
neck (of the bottle, etc.)	**leher**	[leher]

carafe (decanter)	**karaf**	[karaf]
pitcher	**kendi**	[kendi]
vessel (container)	**wadah**	[wadah]
pot (crock, stoneware ~)	**pot**	[pot]
vase	**vas**	[vas]

flacon, bottle (perfume ~)	**botol**	[botol]
vial, small bottle	**botol kecil**	[botol ketʃil]
tube (of toothpaste)	**tabung**	[tabuŋ]

sack (bag)	**karung**	[karuŋ]
bag (paper ~, plastic ~)	**kantong**	[kantoŋ]
packet (of cigarettes, etc.)	**bungkus**	[buŋkus]

box (e.g. shoebox)	**kotak, kardus**	[kotak], [kardus]
crate	**kotak**	[kotaʔ]
basket	**bakul**	[bakul]

24. Materials

material	**bahan**	[bahan]
wood (n)	**kayu**	[kaju]
wood-, wooden (adj)	**kayu**	[kaju]

glass (n)	**kaca**	[katʃa]
glass (as adj)	**kaca**	[katʃa]

stone (n)	**batu**	[batu]
stone (as adj)	**batu**	[batu]

plastic (n)	**plastik**	[plastiʔ]
plastic (as adj)	**plastik**	[plastiʔ]

rubber (n)	**karet**	[karet]
rubber (as adj)	**karet**	[karet]

cloth, fabric (n)	**kain**	[kain]
fabric (as adj)	**kain**	[kain]

paper (n)	**kertas**	[kertas]
paper (as adj)	**kertas**	[kertas]

cardboard (n)	**karton**	[karton]
cardboard (as adj)	**karton**	[karton]
polyethylene	**polietilena**	[polietilena]
cellophane	**selofana**	[selofana]

| linoleum | linoleum | [linoleum] |
| plywood | kayu lapis | [kaju lapis] |

porcelain (n)	porselen	[porselen]
porcelain (as adj)	porselen	[porselen]
clay (n)	tanah liat	[tanah liat]
clay (as adj)	gerabah	[gerabah]
ceramic (n)	keramik	[kerami']
ceramic (as adj)	keramik	[kerami']

25. Metals

metal (n)	logam	[logam]
metal (as adj)	logam	[logam]
alloy (n)	aloi, lakur	[aloy], [lakur]

gold (n)	emas	[emas]
gold, golden (adj)	emas	[emas]
silver (n)	perak	[pera']
silver (as adj)	perak	[pera']

iron (n)	besi	[besi]
iron-, made of iron (adj)	besi	[besi]
steel (n)	baja	[badʒʲa]
steel (as adj)	baja	[badʒʲa]
copper (n)	tembaga	[tembaga]
copper (as adj)	tembaga	[tembaga]

aluminium (n)	aluminium	[aluminium]
aluminium (as adj)	aluminium	[aluminium]
bronze (n)	perunggu	[pəruŋgu]
bronze (as adj)	perunggu	[pəruŋgu]

brass	kuningan	[kuniŋan]
nickel	nikel	[nikel]
platinum	platinum	[platinum]
mercury	air raksa	[air raksa]
tin	timah	[timah]
lead	timbal	[timbal]
zinc	seng	[seŋ]

HUMAN BEING

Human being. The body

26. Humans. Basic concepts

human being	**manusia**	[manusia]
man (adult male)	**laki-laki, pria**	[laki-laki], [pria]
woman	**perempuan, wanita**	[pərempuan], [wanita]
child	**anak**	[anaʔ]
girl	**anak perempuan**	[anaʔ pərempuan]
boy	**anak laki-laki**	[anaʔ laki-laki]
teenager	**remaja**	[remadʒʲa]
old man	**lelaki tua**	[lelaki tua]
old woman	**perempuan tua**	[pərempuan tua]

27. Human anatomy

organism (body)	**organisme**	[organisme]
heart	**jantung**	[dʒʲantuŋ]
blood	**darah**	[darah]
artery	**arteri, pembuluh darah**	[arteri], [pembuluh darah]
vein	**vena**	[vena]
brain	**otak**	[otaʔ]
nerve	**saraf**	[saraf]
nerves	**saraf**	[saraf]
vertebra	**ruas**	[ruas]
spine (backbone)	**tulang belakang**	[tulaŋ belakaŋ]
stomach (organ)	**lambung**	[lambuŋ]
intestines, bowels	**usus**	[usus]
intestine (e.g. large ~)	**usus**	[usus]
liver	**hati**	[hati]
kidney	**ginjal**	[gindʒʲal]
bone	**tulang**	[tulaŋ]
skeleton	**skelet, rangka**	[skelet], [raŋka]
rib	**tulang rusuk**	[tulaŋ rusuʔ]
skull	**tengkorak**	[teŋkoraʔ]
muscle	**otot**	[otot]
biceps	**bisep**	[bisep]
triceps	**trisep**	[trisep]
tendon	**tendon**	[tendon]
joint	**sendi**	[sendi]

lungs	paru-paru	[paru-paru]
genitals	kemaluan	[kemaluan]
skin	kulit	[kulit]

28. Head

head	kepala	[kepala]
face	wajah	[wadʒ'ah]
nose	hidung	[hiduŋ]
mouth	mulut	[mulut]

eye	mata	[mata]
eyes	mata	[mata]
pupil	pupil, biji mata	[pupil], [bidʒi mata]
eyebrow	alis	[alis]
eyelash	bulu mata	[bulu mata]
eyelid	kelopak mata	[kelopa' mata]

tongue	lidah	[lidah]
tooth	gigi	[gigi]
lips	bibir	[bibir]
cheekbones	tulang pipi	[tulaŋ pipi]
gum	gusi	[gusi]
palate	langit-langit mulut	[laŋit-laŋit mulut]

nostrils	lubang hidung	[lubaŋ hiduŋ]
chin	dagu	[dagu]
jaw	rahang	[rahaŋ]
cheek	pipi	[pipi]

forehead	dahi	[dahi]
temple	pelipis	[pelipis]
ear	telinga	[teliŋa]
back of the head	tengkuk	[teŋku']
neck	leher	[leher]
throat	tenggorok	[teŋgoro']

hair	rambut	[rambut]
hairstyle	tatanan rambut	[tatanan rambut]
haircut	potongan rambut	[potoŋan rambut]
wig	wig, rambut palsu	[wig], [rambut palsu]

moustache	kumis	[kumis]
beard	janggut	[dʒ'aŋgut]
to have (a beard, etc.)	memelihara	[memelihara]
plait	kepang	[kepaŋ]
sideboards	brewok	[brewo']

red-haired (adj)	merah pirang	[merah piraŋ]
grey (hair)	beruban	[bəruban]
bald (adj)	botak, plontos	[botak], [plontos]
bald patch	botak	[bota']
ponytail	ekor kuda	[ekor kuda]
fringe	poni rambut	[poni rambut]

29. Human body

| hand | **tangan** | [taŋan] |
| arm | **lengan** | [leŋan] |

finger	**jari**	[dʒari]
toe	**jari**	[dʒari]
thumb	**jempol**	[dʒempol]
little finger	**jari kelingking**	[dʒari keliŋkiŋ]
nail	**kuku**	[kuku]

fist	**kepalan tangan**	[kepalan taŋan]
palm	**telapak**	[telapaʔ]
wrist	**pergelangan**	[pergelaŋan]
forearm	**lengan bawah**	[leŋan bawah]
elbow	**siku**	[siku]
shoulder	**bahu**	[bahu]

leg	**kaki**	[kaki]
foot	**telapak kaki**	[telapaʔ kaki]
knee	**lutut**	[lutut]
calf	**betis**	[betis]
hip	**paha**	[paha]
heel	**tumit**	[tumit]

body	**tubuh**	[tubuh]
stomach	**perut**	[perut]
chest	**dada**	[dada]
breast	**payudara**	[pajudara]
flank	**rusuk**	[rusuʔ]
back	**punggung**	[puŋguŋ]
lower back	**pinggang bawah**	[piŋgaŋ bawah]
waist	**pinggang**	[piŋgaŋ]

navel (belly button)	**pusar**	[pusar]
buttocks	**pantat**	[pantat]
bottom	**pantat**	[pantat]

beauty spot	**tanda lahir**	[tanda lahir]
birthmark (café au lait spot)	**tanda lahir**	[tanda lahir]
tattoo	**tato**	[tato]
scar	**parut luka**	[parut luka]

Clothing & Accessories

30. Outerwear. Coats

clothes	**pakaian**	[pakajan]
outerwear	**pakaian luar**	[pakajan luar]
winter clothing	**pakaian musim dingin**	[pakajan musim diɲin]
coat (overcoat)	**mantel**	[mantel]
fur coat	**mantel bulu**	[mantel bulu]
fur jacket	**jaket bulu**	[dʒʲaket bulu]
down coat	**jaket bulu halus**	[dʒʲaket bulu halus]
jacket (e.g. leather ~)	**jaket**	[dʒʲaket]
raincoat (trenchcoat, etc.)	**jas hujan**	[dʒʲas hudʒʲan]
waterproof (adj)	**kedap air**	[kedap air]

31. Men's & women's clothing

shirt (button shirt)	**kemeja**	[kemedʒʲa]
trousers	**celana**	[ʧelana]
jeans	**celana jins**	[ʧelana dʒins]
suit jacket	**jas**	[dʒʲas]
suit	**setelan**	[setelan]
dress (frock)	**gaun**	[gaun]
skirt	**rok**	[roʔ]
blouse	**blus**	[blus]
knitted jacket (cardigan, etc.)	**jaket wol**	[dʒʲaket wol]
jacket (of a woman's suit)	**jaket**	[dʒʲaket]
T-shirt	**baju kaus**	[badʒʲu kaus]
shorts (short trousers)	**celana pendek**	[ʧelana pendeʔ]
tracksuit	**pakaian olahraga**	[pakajan olahraga]
bathrobe	**jubah mandi**	[dʒʲubah mandi]
pyjamas	**piyama**	[piyama]
jumper (sweater)	**sweter**	[sweter]
pullover	**pulover**	[pulover]
waistcoat	**rompi**	[rompi]
tailcoat	**jas berbuntut**	[dʒʲas berbuntut]
dinner suit	**jas malam**	[dʒʲas malam]
uniform	**seragam**	[seragam]
workwear	**pakaian kerja**	[pakajan kerdʒʲa]
boiler suit	**baju monyet**	[badʒʲu monjet]
coat (e.g. doctor's smock)	**jas**	[dʒʲas]

32. Clothing. Underwear

underwear	**pakaian dalam**	[pakajan dalam]
pants	**celana dalam lelaki**	[ʧelana dalam lelaki]
panties	**celana dalam wanita**	[ʧelana dalam wanita]
vest (singlet)	**singlet**	[siŋlet]
socks	**kaus kaki**	[kaus kaki]
nightdress	**baju tidur**	[baʤʲu tidur]
bra	**beha**	[beha]
knee highs (knee-high socks)	**kaus kaki selutut**	[kaus kaki selutut]
tights	**pantihos**	[pantihos]
stockings (hold ups)	**kaus kaki panjang**	[kaus kaki panʤʲaŋ]
swimsuit, bikini	**baju renang**	[baʤʲu renaŋ]

33. Headwear

hat	**topi**	[topi]
trilby hat	**topi bulat**	[topi bulat]
baseball cap	**topi bisbol**	[topi bisbol]
flatcap	**topi pet**	[topi pet]
beret	**baret**	[baret]
hood	**kerudung kepala**	[keruduŋ kepala]
panama hat	**topi panama**	[topi panama]
knit cap (knitted hat)	**topi rajut**	[topi raʤʲut]
headscarf	**tudung kepala**	[tuduŋ kepala]
women's hat	**topi wanita**	[topi wanita]
hard hat	**topi baja**	[topi baʤʲa]
forage cap	**topi lipat**	[topi lipat]
helmet	**helm**	[helm]
bowler	**topi bulat**	[topi bulat]
top hat	**topi tinggi**	[topi tiŋgi]

34. Footwear

footwear	**sepatu**	[sepatu]
shoes (men's shoes)	**sepatu bot**	[sepatu bot]
shoes (women's shoes)	**sepatu wanita**	[sepatu wanita]
boots (e.g., cowboy ~)	**sepatu lars**	[sepatu lars]
carpet slippers	**pantofel**	[pantofel]
trainers	**sepatu tenis**	[sepatu tenis]
trainers	**sepatu kets**	[sepatu kets]
sandals	**sandal**	[sandal]
cobbler (shoe repairer)	**tukang sepatu**	[tukaŋ sepatu]
heel	**tumit**	[tumit]

pair (of shoes)	sepasang	[sepasaŋ]
lace (shoelace)	tali sepatu	[tali sepatu]
to lace up (vt)	mengikat tali	[məŋikat tali]
shoehorn	sendok sepatu	[sendo' sepatu]
shoe polish	semir sepatu	[semir sepatu]

35. Textile. Fabrics

cotton (n)	katun	[katun]
cotton (as adj)	katun	[katun]
flax (n)	linen	[linen]
flax (as adj)	linen	[linen]

silk (n)	sutra	[sutra]
silk (as adj)	sutra	[sutra]
wool (n)	wol	[wol]
wool (as adj)	wol	[wol]

velvet	beledu	[beledu]
suede	suede	[suede]
corduroy	korduroi	[korduroy]

nylon (n)	nilon	[nilon]
nylon (as adj)	nilon	[nilon]
polyester (n)	poliester	[poliester]
polyester (as adj)	poliester	[poliester]

leather (n)	kulit	[kulit]
leather (as adj)	kulit	[kulit]
fur (n)	kulit berbulu	[kulit bərbulu]
fur (e.g. ~ coat)	bulu	[bulu]

36. Personal accessories

gloves	sarung tangan	[saruŋ taŋan]
mittens	sarung tangan	[saruŋ taŋan]
scarf (muffler)	selendang	[selendaŋ]

glasses	kacamata	[katʃamata]
frame (eyeglass ~)	bingkai	[biŋkaj]
umbrella	payung	[pajuŋ]
walking stick	tongkat jalan	[toŋkat dʒʲalan]
hairbrush	sikat rambut	[sikat rambut]
fan	kipas	[kipas]

tie (necktie)	dasi	[dasi]
bow tie	dasi kupu-kupu	[dasi kupu-kupu]
braces	bretel	[bretel]
handkerchief	sapu tangan	[sapu taŋan]

| comb | sisir | [sisir] |
| hair slide | jepit rambut | [dʒʲepit rambut] |

| hairpin | harnal | [harnal] |
| buckle | gesper | [gesper] |

| belt | sabuk | [sabuʔ] |
| shoulder strap | tali tas | [tali tas] |

bag (handbag)	tas	[tas]
handbag	tas tangan	[tas taŋan]
rucksack	ransel	[ransel]

37. Clothing. Miscellaneous

fashion	mode	[mode]
in vogue (adj)	modis	[modis]
fashion designer	perancang busana	[pərantʃaŋ busana]

collar	kerah	[kerah]
pocket	saku	[saku]
pocket (as adj)	saku	[saku]
sleeve	lengan	[leŋan]
hanging loop	tali kait	[tali kait]
flies (on trousers)	golbi	[golbi]

zip (fastener)	ritsleting	[ritsletiŋ]
fastener	kancing	[kantʃiŋ]
button	kancing	[kantʃiŋ]
buttonhole	lubang kancing	[lubaŋ kantʃiŋ]
to come off (ab. button)	terlepas	[tərlepas]

to sew (vi, vt)	menjahit	[məndʒʲahit]
to embroider (vi, vt)	membordir	[membordir]
embroidery	bordiran	[bordiran]
sewing needle	jarum	[dʒʲarum]
thread	benang	[benaŋ]
seam	setik	[setiʔ]

to get dirty (vi)	kena kotor	[kena kotor]
stain (mark, spot)	bercak	[bertʃaʔ]
to crease, to crumple	kumal	[kumal]
to tear, to rip (vt)	merobek	[merobeʔ]
clothes moth	ngengat	[ŋeŋat]

38. Personal care. Cosmetics

toothpaste	pasta gigi	[pasta gigi]
toothbrush	sikat gigi	[sikat gigi]
to clean one's teeth	menggosok gigi	[məŋgoso' gigi]

razor	pisau cukur	[pisau tʃukur]
shaving cream	krim cukur	[krim tʃukur]
to shave (vi)	bercukur	[bərtʃukur]
soap	sabun	[sabun]

shampoo	sampo	[sampo]
scissors	gunting	[guntiŋ]
nail file	kikir kuku	[kikir kuku]
nail clippers	pemotong kuku	[pemotoŋ kuku]
tweezers	pinset	[pinset]

cosmetics	kosmetik	[kosmetiʔ]
face mask	masker	[masker]
manicure	manikur	[manikur]
to have a manicure	melakukan manikur	[melakukan manikur]
pedicure	pedi	[pedi]

make-up bag	tas kosmetik	[tas kosmetiʔ]
face powder	bedak	[bedaʔ]
powder compact	kotak bedak	[kotaʔ bedaʔ]
blusher	perona pipi	[pərona pipi]

perfume (bottled)	parfum	[parfum]
toilet water (lotion)	minyak wangi	[minjaʔ waŋi]
lotion	losion	[losjon]
cologne	kolonye	[kolone]

eyeshadow	pewarna mata	[pewarna mata]
eyeliner	pensil alis	[pensil alis]
mascara	celak	[tʃelaʔ]

lipstick	lipstik	[lipstiʔ]
nail polish	kuteks, cat kuku	[kuteks], [tʃat kuku]
hair spray	semprotan rambut	[semprotan rambut]
deodorant	deodoran	[deodoran]

cream	krim	[krim]
face cream	krim wajah	[krim wadʒⁱah]
hand cream	krim tangan	[krim taŋan]
anti-wrinkle cream	krim antikerut	[krim antikerut]
day cream	krim siang	[krim siaŋ]
night cream	krim malam	[krim malam]
day (as adj)	siang	[siaŋ]
night (as adj)	malam	[malam]

tampon	tampon	[tampon]
toilet paper (toilet roll)	kertas toilet	[kertas toylet]
hair dryer	pengering rambut	[peŋeriŋ rambut]

39. Jewellery

jewellery, jewels	perhiasan	[pərhiasan]
precious (e.g. ~ stone)	mulia, berharga	[mulia], [berharga]
hallmark stamp	tanda kadar	[tanda kadar]

ring	cincin	[tʃintʃin]
wedding ring	cincin kawin	[tʃintʃin kawin]
bracelet	gelang	[gelaŋ]
earrings	anting-anting	[antiŋ-antiŋ]

necklace (~ of pearls)	kalung	[kaluŋ]
crown	mahkota	[mahkota]
bead necklace	kalung manik-manik	[kaluŋ maniʔ-maniʔ]

diamond	berlian	[bərlian]
emerald	zamrud	[zamrud]
ruby	batu mirah delima	[batu mirah delima]
sapphire	nilakandi	[nilakandi]
pearl	mutiara	[mutiara]
amber	batu amber	[batu amber]

40. Watches. Clocks

watch (wristwatch)	arloji	[arlodʒi]
dial	piringan jam	[piriŋan dʒʲam]
hand (clock, watch)	jarum	[dʒʲarum]
metal bracelet	rantai arloji	[rantaj arlodʒi]
watch strap	tali arloji	[tali arlodʒi]

battery	baterai	[bateraj]
to be flat (battery)	mati	[mati]
to change a battery	mengganti baterai	[məŋganti bateraj]
to run fast	cepat	[tʃepat]
to run slow	terlambat	[tərlambat]

wall clock	jam dinding	[dʒʲam dindiŋ]
hourglass	jam pasir	[dʒʲam pasir]
sundial	jam matahari	[dʒʲam matahari]
alarm clock	weker	[weker]
watchmaker	tukang jam	[tukaŋ dʒʲam]
to repair (vt)	mereparasi, memperbaiki	[mereparasi], [memperbajki]

Food. Nutricion

meat	daging	[dagiŋ]
chicken	ayam	[ajam]
poussin	anak ayam	[ana' ajam]
duck	bebek	[bebeʔ]
goose	angsa	[aŋsa]
game	binatang buruan	[binataŋ buruan]
turkey	kalkun	[kalkun]

pork	daging babi	[dagiŋ babi]
veal	daging anak sapi	[dagiŋ ana' sapi]
lamb	daging domba	[dagiŋ domba]
beef	daging sapi	[dagiŋ sapi]
rabbit	kelinci	[kelintʃi]

sausage (bologna, etc.)	sosis	[sosis]
vienna sausage (frankfurter)	sosis	[sosis]
bacon	bakon	[beykon]
ham	ham, daging kornet	[ham], [dagiŋ kornet]
gammon	ham	[ham]

pâté	pasta	[pasta]
liver	hati	[hati]
mince (minced meat)	daging giling	[dagiŋ giliŋ]
tongue	lidah	[lidah]

egg	telur	[telur]
eggs	telur	[telur]
egg white	putih telur	[putih telur]
egg yolk	kuning telur	[kuniŋ telur]

fish	ikan	[ikan]
seafood	makanan laut	[makanan laut]
crustaceans	krustasea	[krustasea]
caviar	caviar	[kaviar]

crab	kepiting	[kepitiŋ]
prawn	udang	[udaŋ]
oyster	tiram	[tiram]
spiny lobster	lobster berduri	[lobster bərduri]
octopus	gurita	[gurita]
squid	cumi-cumi	[tʃumi-tʃumi]

sturgeon	ikan sturgeon	[ikan sturdʒˈen]
salmon	salmon	[salmon]
halibut	ikan turbot	[ikan turbot]
cod	ikan kod	[ikan kod]

mackerel	ikan kembung	[ikan kembuŋ]
tuna	tuna	[tuna]
eel	belut	[belut]

trout	ikan forel	[ikan forel]
sardine	sarden	[sarden]
pike	ikan pike	[ikan paik]
herring	ikan haring	[ikan hariŋ]

bread	roti	[roti]
cheese	keju	[kedʒʲu]
sugar	gula	[gula]
salt	garam	[garam]

rice	beras, nasi	[beras], [nasi]
pasta (macaroni)	makaroni	[makaroni]
noodles	mi	[mi]

butter	mentega	[məntega]
vegetable oil	minyak nabati	[minja' nabati]
sunflower oil	minyak bunga matahari	[minja' buŋa matahari]
margarine	margarin	[margarin]

| olives | buah zaitun | [buah zajtun] |
| olive oil | minyak zaitun | [minja' zajtun] |

milk	susu	[susu]
condensed milk	susu kental	[susu kental]
yogurt	yogurt	[yogurt]
soured cream	krim asam	[krim asam]
cream (of milk)	krim, kepala susu	[krim], [kepala susu]

| mayonnaise | mayones | [majones] |
| buttercream | krim | [krim] |

groats (barley ~, etc.)	menir	[menir]
flour	tepung	[tepuŋ]
tinned food	makanan kalengan	[makanan kaleŋan]

cornflakes	emping jagung	[empiŋ dʒʲaguŋ]
honey	madu	[madu]
jam	selai	[selaj]
chewing gum	permen karet	[pərmen karet]

42. Drinks

water	air	[air]
drinking water	air minum	[air minum]
mineral water	air mineral	[air mineral]

still (adj)	tanpa gas	[tanpa gas]
carbonated (adj)	berkarbonasi	[bərkarbonasi]
sparkling (adj)	bergas	[bərgas]
ice	es	[es]

with ice	dengan es	[deŋan es]
non-alcoholic (adj)	tanpa alkohol	[tanpa alkohol]
soft drink	minuman ringan	[minuman riŋan]
refreshing drink	minuman penygar	[minuman penigar]
lemonade	limun	[limun]
spirits	minoman beralkohol	[minoman bəralkohol]
wine	anggur	[aŋgur]
white wine	anggur putih	[aŋgur putih]
red wine	anggur merah	[aŋgur merah]
liqueur	likeur	[likeur]
champagne	sampanye	[sampanje]
vermouth	vermouth	[vermut]
whisky	wiski	[wiski]
vodka	vodka	[vodka]
gin	jin, jenewer	[dʒin], [dʒʲenewer]
cognac	konyak	[konjaʔ]
rum	rum	[rum]
coffee	kopi	[kopi]
black coffee	kopi pahit	[kopi pahit]
white coffee	kopi susu	[kopi susu]
cappuccino	cappuccino	[kaputʃino]
instant coffee	kopi instan	[kopi instan]
milk	susu	[susu]
cocktail	koktail	[koktajl]
milkshake	susu kocok	[susu kotʃoʔ]
juice	jus	[dʒʲus]
tomato juice	jus tomat	[dʒʲus tomat]
orange juice	jus jeruk	[dʒʲus dʒʲeruʔ]
freshly squeezed juice	jus peras	[dʒʲus pəras]
beer	bir	[bir]
lager	bir putih	[bir putih]
bitter	bir hitam	[bir hitam]
tea	teh	[teh]
black tea	teh hitam	[teh hitam]
green tea	teh hijau	[teh hidʒʲau]

43. Vegetables

vegetables	sayuran	[sajuran]
greens	sayuran hijau	[sajuran hidʒʲau]
tomato	tomat	[tomat]
cucumber	mentimun, ketimun	[məntimun], [ketimun]
carrot	wortel	[wortel]
potato	kentang	[kentaŋ]
onion	bawang	[bawaŋ]

garlic	**bawang putih**	[bawaŋ putih]
cabbage	**kol**	[kol]
cauliflower	**kembang kol**	[kembaŋ kol]
Brussels sprouts	**kol Brussels**	[kol brusels]
broccoli	**brokoli**	[brokoli]

beetroot	**ubi bit merah**	[ubi bit merah]
aubergine	**terung, terong**	[teruŋ], [teroŋ]
courgette	**labu siam**	[labu siam]
pumpkin	**labu**	[labu]
turnip	**turnip**	[turnip]

parsley	**peterseli**	[peterseli]
dill	**adas sowa**	[adas sowa]
lettuce	**selada**	[selada]
celery	**seledri**	[seledri]
asparagus	**asparagus**	[asparagus]
spinach	**bayam**	[bajam]

pea	**kacang polong**	[katʃaŋ poloŋ]
beans	**kacang-kacangan**	[katʃaŋ-katʃaŋan]
maize	**jagung**	[dʒˈaguŋ]
kidney bean	**kacang buncis**	[katʃaŋ buntʃis]

sweet paper	**cabai**	[tʃabaj]
radish	**radis**	[radis]
artichoke	**artisyok**	[artiʃoˀ]

44. Fruits. Nuts

fruit	**buah**	[buah]
apple	**apel**	[apel]
pear	**pir**	[pir]
lemon	**jeruk sitrun**	[dʒˈeruˀ sitrun]
orange	**jeruk manis**	[dʒˈeruˀ manis]
strawberry (garden ~)	**stroberi**	[stroberi]

tangerine	**jeruk mandarin**	[dʒˈeruˀ mandarin]
plum	**plum**	[plum]
peach	**persik**	[persiˀ]
apricot	**aprikot**	[aprikot]
raspberry	**buah frambus**	[buah frambus]
pineapple	**nanas**	[nanas]

banana	**pisang**	[pisaŋ]
watermelon	**semangka**	[semaŋka]
grape	**buah anggur**	[buah aŋgur]
sour cherry	**buah ceri asam**	[buah tʃeri asam]
sweet cherry	**buah ceri manis**	[buah tʃeri manis]
melon	**melon**	[melon]

grapefruit	**jeruk Bali**	[dʒˈeruˀ bali]
avocado	**avokad**	[avokad]
papaya	**pepaya**	[pepaja]

mango	mangga	[maŋga]
pomegranate	buah delima	[buah delima]

redcurrant	redcurrant	[redkaren]
blackcurrant	blackcurrant	[ble'karen]
gooseberry	buah arbei hijau	[buah arbei hidʒiau]
bilberry	buah bilberi	[buah bilberi]
blackberry	beri hitam	[beri hitam]

raisin	kismis	[kismis]
fig	buah ara	[buah ara]
date	buah kurma	[buah kurma]

peanut	kacang tanah	[katʃaŋ tanah]
almond	badam	[badam]
walnut	buah walnut	[buah walnut]
hazelnut	kacang hazel	[katʃaŋ hazel]
coconut	buah kelapa	[buah kelapa]
pistachios	badam hijau	[badam hidʒiau]

45. Bread. Sweets

bakers' confectionery (pastry)	kue-mue	[kue-mue]
bread	roti	[roti]
biscuits	biskuit	[biskuit]

chocolate (n)	cokelat	[tʃokelat]
chocolate (as adj)	cokelat	[tʃokelat]
candy (wrapped)	permen	[pərmen]
cake (e.g. cupcake)	kue	[kue]
cake (e.g. birthday ~)	kue tar	[kue tar]

pie (e.g. apple ~)	pai	[pai]
filling (for cake, pie)	inti	[inti]

jam (whole fruit jam)	selai buah utuh	[selaj buah utuh]
marmalade	marmelade	[marmelade]
wafers	wafel	[wafel]
ice-cream	es krim	[es krim]
pudding (Christmas ~)	puding	[pudiŋ]

46. Cooked dishes

course, dish	masakan, hidangan	[masakan], [hidaŋan]
cuisine	masakan	[masakan]
recipe	resep	[resep]
portion	porsi	[porsi]

salad	salada	[salada]
soup	sup	[sup]
clear soup (broth)	kaldu	[kaldu]
sandwich (bread)	roti lapis	[roti lapis]

fried eggs	telur mata sapi	[telur mata sapi]
hamburger (beefburger)	hamburger	[hamburger]
beefsteak	bistik	[bisti']

side dish	lauk	[lau']
spaghetti	spageti	[spageti]
mash	kentang tumbuk	[kentaŋ tumbu']
pizza	piza	[piza]
porridge (oatmeal, etc.)	bubur	[bubur]
omelette	telur dadar	[telur dadar]

boiled (e.g. ~ beef)	rebus	[rebus]
smoked (adj)	asap	[asap]
fried (adj)	goreng	[goreŋ]
dried (adj)	kering	[keriŋ]
frozen (adj)	beku	[beku]
pickled (adj)	marinade	[marinade]

sweet (sugary)	manis	[manis]
salty (adj)	asin	[asin]
cold (adj)	dingin	[diŋin]
hot (adj)	panas	[panas]
bitter (adj)	pahit	[pahit]
tasty (adj)	enak	[ena']

to cook in boiling water	merebus	[merebus]
to cook (dinner)	memasak	[memasa']
to fry (vt)	menggoreng	[məŋgoreŋ]
to heat up (food)	memanaskan	[memanaskan]

to salt (vt)	menggarami	[məŋgarami]
to pepper (vt)	membubuh merica	[membubuh meritʃa]
to grate (vt)	memarut	[memarut]
peel (n)	kulit	[kulit]
to peel (vt)	mengupas	[məŋupas]

47. Spices

salt	garam	[garam]
salty (adj)	asin	[asin]
to salt (vt)	menggarami	[məŋgarami]

black pepper	merica	[meritʃa]
red pepper (milled ~)	cabai merah	[tʃabaj merah]
mustard	mustar	[mustar]
horseradish	lobak pedas	[loba' pedas]

condiment	bumbu	[bumbu]
spice	rempah-rempah	[rempah-rempah]
sauce	saus	[saus]
vinegar	cuka	[tʃuka]

| anise | adas manis | [adas manis] |
| basil | selasih | [selasih] |

cloves	cengkih	[tʃeŋkih]
ginger	jahe	[dʒʲahe]
coriander	ketumbar	[ketumbar]
cinnamon	kayu manis	[kaju manis]

sesame	wijen	[widʒʲen]
bay leaf	daun salam	[daun salam]
paprika	cabai	[tʃabaj]
caraway	jintan	[dʒintan]
saffron	kuma-kuma	[kuma-kuma]

48. Meals

| food | makanan | [makanan] |
| to eat (vi, vt) | makan | [makan] |

breakfast	makan pagi, sarapan	[makan pagi], [sarapan]
to have breakfast	sarapan	[sarapan]
lunch	makan siang	[makan siaŋ]
to have lunch	makan siang	[makan siaŋ]
dinner	makan malam	[makan malam]
to have dinner	makan malam	[makan malam]

| appetite | nafsu makan | [nafsu makan] |
| Enjoy your meal! | Selamat makan! | [selamat makan!] |

| to open (~ a bottle) | membuka | [membuka] |
| to spill (liquid) | menumpahkan | [mənumpahkan] |

to boil (vi)	mendidih	[məndidih]
to boil (vt)	mendidihkan	[məndidihkan]
boiled (~ water)	masak	[masaʔ]

| to chill, cool down (vt) | mendinginkan | [məndiɲinkan] |
| to chill (vi) | mendingin | [məndiŋin] |

| taste, flavour | rasa | [rasa] |
| aftertaste | nuansa rasa | [nuansa rasa] |

to slim down (lose weight)	berdiet	[berdiet]
diet	diet, pola makan	[diet], [pola makan]
vitamin	vitamin	[vitamin]
calorie	kalori	[kalori]

| vegetarian (n) | vegetarian | [vegetarian] |
| vegetarian (adj) | vegetarian | [vegetarian] |

fats (nutrient)	lemak	[lemaʔ]
proteins	protein	[protein]
carbohydrates	karbohidrat	[karbohidrat]

slice (of lemon, ham)	irisan	[irisan]
piece (of cake, pie)	potongan	[potoŋan]
crumb (of bread, cake, etc.)	remah	[remah]

49. Table setting

spoon	**sendok**	[sendo']
knife	**pisau**	[pisau]
fork	**garpu**	[garpu]
cup (e.g., coffee ~)	**cangkir**	[ʧaŋkir]
plate (dinner ~)	**piring**	[piriŋ]
saucer	**alas cangkir**	[alas ʧaŋkir]
serviette	**serbet**	[serbet]
toothpick	**tusuk gigi**	[tusu' gigi]

50. Restaurant

restaurant	**restoran**	[restoran]
coffee bar	**warung kopi**	[waruŋ kopi]
pub, bar	**bar**	[bar]
tearoom	**warung teh**	[waruŋ teh]
waiter	**pelayan lelaki**	[pelajan lelaki]
waitress	**pelayan perempuan**	[pelajan pərempuan]
barman	**pelayan bar**	[pelajan bar]
menu	**menu**	[menu]
wine list	**daftar anggur**	[daftar aŋgur]
to book a table	**memesan meja**	[memesan medʒ'a]
course, dish	**masakan, hidangan**	[masakan], [hidaŋan]
to order (meal)	**memesan**	[memesan]
to make an order	**memesan**	[memesan]
aperitif	**aperitif**	[aperitif]
starter	**makanan ringan**	[makanan riŋan]
dessert, pudding	**hidangan penutup**	[hidaŋan penutup]
bill	**bon**	[bon]
to pay the bill	**membayar bon**	[membajar bon]
to give change	**memberikan uang kembalian**	[memberikan uaŋ kembalian]
tip	**tip**	[tip]

Family, relatives and friends

name (first name)	nama, nama depan	[nama], [nama depan]
surname (last name)	nama keluarga	[nama keluarga]
date of birth	tanggal lahir	[taŋgal lahir]
place of birth	tempat lahir	[tempat lahir]

nationality	kebangsaan	[kebaŋsaʔan]
place of residence	tempat tinggal	[tempat tiŋgal]
country	negara, negeri	[negara], [negeri]
profession (occupation)	profesi	[profesi]

gender, sex	jenis kelamin	[dʒenis kelamin]
height	tinggi badan	[tiŋgi badan]
weight	berat	[berat]

mother	ibu	[ibu]
father	ayah	[ajah]
son	anak lelaki	[anaʔ lelaki]
daughter	anak perempuan	[anaʔ perempuan]

younger daughter	anak perempuan bungsu	[anaʔ perempuan buŋsu]
younger son	anak lelaki bungsu	[anaʔ lelaki buŋsu]
eldest daughter	anak perempuan sulung	[anaʔ perempuan suluŋ]
eldest son	anak lelaki sulung	[anaʔ lelaki suluŋ]

brother	saudara lelaki	[saudara lelaki]
elder brother	kakak lelaki	[kakaʔ lelaki]
younger brother	adik lelaki	[adiʔ lelaki]
sister	saudara perempuan	[saudara perempuan]
elder sister	kakak perempuan	[kakaʔ perempuan]
younger sister	adik perempuan	[adiʔ perempuan]

| cousin (masc.) | sepupu lelaki | [sepupu lelaki] |
| cousin (fem.) | sepupu perempuan | [sepupu perempuan] |

mummy	mama, ibu	[mama], [ibu]
dad, daddy	papa, ayah	[papa], [ajah]
parents	orang tua	[oraŋ tua]
child	anak	[anaʔ]
children	anak-anak	[anaʔ-anaʔ]

| grandmother | nenek | [neneʔ] |
| grandfather | kakek | [kakeʔ] |

grandson	cucu laki-laki	[ʧuʧu laki-laki]
granddaughter	cucu perempuan	[ʧuʧu pərempuan]
grandchildren	cucu	[ʧuʧu]

uncle	paman	[paman]
aunt	bibi	[bibi]
nephew	keponakan laki-laki	[keponakan laki-laki]
niece	keponakan perempuan	[keponakan pərempuan]

mother-in-law (wife's mother)	ibu mertua	[ibu mertua]
father-in-law (husband's father)	ayah mertua	[ajah mertua]
son-in-law (daughter's husband)	menantu laki-laki	[mənantu laki-laki]
stepmother	ibu tiri	[ibu tiri]
stepfather	ayah tiri	[ajah tiri]

infant	bayi	[baji]
baby (infant)	bayi	[baji]
little boy, kid	bocah cilik	[boʧah ʧili']

wife	istri	[istri]
husband	suami	[suami]
spouse (husband)	suami	[suami]
spouse (wife)	istri	[istri]

married (masc.)	menikah, beristri	[mənikah], [bəristri]
married (fem.)	menikah, bersuami	[mənikah], [bərsuami]
single (unmarried)	bujang	[budʒˈaŋ]
bachelor	bujang	[budʒˈaŋ]
divorced (masc.)	bercerai	[bərʧeraj]
widow	janda	[dʒˈanda]
widower	duda	[duda]

relative	kerabat	[kerabat]
close relative	kerabat dekat	[kerabat dekat]
distant relative	kerabat jauh	[kerabat dʒˈauh]
relatives	kerabat, sanak saudara	[kerabat], [sana' saudara]

orphan (boy or girl)	yatim piatu	[yatim piatu]
guardian (of a minor)	wali	[wali]
to adopt (a boy)	mengadopsi	[məŋadopsi]
to adopt (a girl)	mengadopsi	[məŋadopsi]

53. Friends. Colleagues

friend (masc.)	sahabat	[sahabat]
friend (fem.)	sahabat	[sahabat]
friendship	persahabatan	[pərsahabatan]
to be friends	bersahabat	[bərsahabat]

| pal (masc.) | teman | [teman] |
| pal (fem.) | teman | [teman] |

partner	**mitra**	[mitra]
chief (boss)	**atasan**	[atasan]
superior (n)	**atasan**	[atasan]
owner, proprietor	**pemilik**	[pemili']
subordinate (n)	**bawahan**	[bawahan]
colleague	**kolega**	[kolega]
acquaintance (person)	**kenalan**	[kenalan]
fellow traveller	**rekan seperjalanan**	[rekan seperdʒ¡alanan]
classmate	**teman sekelas**	[teman sekelas]
neighbour (masc.)	**tetangga**	[tetaŋga]
neighbour (fem.)	**tetangga**	[tetaŋga]
neighbours	**para tetangga**	[para tetaŋga]

54. Man. Woman

woman	**perempuan, wanita**	[pərempuan], [wanita]
girl (young woman)	**gadis**	[gadis]
bride	**mempelai perempuan**	[mempelaj pərempuan]
beautiful (adj)	**cantik**	[tʃanti']
tall (adj)	**tinggi**	[tiŋgi]
slender (adj)	**ramping**	[rampiŋ]
short (adj)	**pendek**	[pende']
blonde (n)	**orang berambut pirang**	[oraŋ bərambut piraŋ]
brunette (n)	**orang berambut cokelat**	[oraŋ bərambut tʃokelat]
ladies' (adj)	**wanita**	[wanita]
virgin (girl)	**perawan**	[pərawan]
pregnant (adj)	**hamil**	[hamil]
man (adult male)	**laki-laki, pria**	[laki-laki], [pria]
blonde haired man	**orang berambut pirang**	[oraŋ bərambut piraŋ]
dark haired man	**orang berambut cokelat**	[oraŋ bərambut tʃokelat]
tall (adj)	**tinggi**	[tiŋgi]
short (adj)	**pendek**	[pende']
rude (rough)	**kasar**	[kasar]
stocky (adj)	**kekar**	[kekar]
robust (adj)	**tegap**	[tegap]
strong (adj)	**kuat**	[kuat]
strength	**kekuatan**	[kekuatan]
plump, fat (adj)	**gemuk**	[gemu']
swarthy (dark-skinned)	**berkulit hitam**	[bərkulit hitam]
slender (well-built)	**ramping**	[rampiŋ]
elegant (adj)	**anggun**	[aŋgun]

55. Age

age	**umur**	[umur]
youth (young age)	**usia muda**	[usia muda]

young (adj)	muda	[muda]
younger (adj)	lebih muda	[lebih muda]
older (adj)	lebih tua	[lebih tua]

young man	pemuda	[pemuda]
teenager	remaja	[remadʒ'a]
guy, fellow	cowok	[tʃowoʔ]

| old man | lelaki tua | [lelaki tua] |
| old woman | perempuan tua | [pərempuan tua] |

adult (adj)	dewasa	[dewasa]
middle-aged (adj)	paruh baya	[paruh baja]
elderly (adj)	lansia	[lansia]
old (adj)	tua	[tua]

retirement	pensiun	[pensiun]
to retire (from job)	pensiun	[pensiun]
retiree, pensioner	pensiunan	[pensiunan]

56. Children

child	anak	[anaʔ]
children	anak-anak	[anaʔ-anaʔ]
twins	kembar	[kembar]

cradle	buaian	[buajan]
rattle	ocehan	[otʃehan]
nappy	popok	[popoʔ]

dummy, comforter	dot	[dot]
pram	kereta bayi	[kereta baji]
nursery	taman kanak-kanak	[taman kanaʔ-kanaʔ]
babysitter	pengasuh anak	[peŋasuh anaʔ]

childhood	masa kanak-kanak	[masa kanaʔ-kanaʔ]
doll	boneka	[boneka]
toy	mainan	[majnan]
construction set (toy)	alat permainan bongkah	[alat pərmajnan boŋkah]
well-bred (adj)	beradab	[bəradab]
ill-bred (adj)	biadab	[biadab]
spoilt (adj)	manja	[mandʒ'a]

to be naughty	nakal	[nakal]
mischievous (adj)	nakal	[nakal]
mischievousness	kenakalan	[kenakalan]
mischievous child	anak nakal	[anaʔ nakal]

| obedient (adj) | patuh | [patuh] |
| disobedient (adj) | tidak patuh | [tidaʔ patuh] |

docile (adj)	penurut	[penurut]
clever (intelligent)	pandai, pintar	[pandaj], [pintar]
child prodigy	anak ajaib	[anaʔ adʒ'ajb]

57. Married couples. Family life

to kiss (vt)	mencium	[məntʃium]
to kiss (vi)	berciuman	[bərtʃiuman]
family (n)	keluarga	[keluarga]
family (as adj)	keluarga	[keluarga]
couple	pasangan	[pasaŋan]
marriage (state)	pernikahan	[pərnikahan]
hearth (home)	rumah tangga	[rumah taŋga]
dynasty	dinasti	[dinasti]
date	kencan	[kentʃan]
kiss	ciuman	[tʃiuman]
love (for sb)	cinta	[tʃinta]
to love (sb)	mencintai	[məntʃintaj]
beloved	kekasih	[kekasih]
tenderness	kelembutan	[kelembutan]
tender (affectionate)	lembut	[lembut]
faithfulness	kesetiaan	[kesetia'an]
faithful (adj)	setia	[setia]
care (attention)	perhatian	[pərhatian]
caring (~ father)	penuh perhatian	[penuh pərhatian]
newlyweds	pengantin baru	[peŋantin baru]
honeymoon	bulan madu	[bulan madu]
to get married (ab. woman)	menikah, bersuami	[mənikah], [bərsuami]
to get married (ab. man)	menikah, beristri	[mənikah], [bəristri]
wedding	pernikahan	[pərnikahan]
golden wedding	pernikahan emas	[pərnikahan emas]
anniversary	hari jadi, HUT	[hari dʒ'adi], [ha-u-te]
lover (masc.)	pria idaman lain	[pria idaman lajn]
mistress (lover)	wanita idaman lain	[wanita idaman lajn]
adultery	perselingkuhan	[pərseliŋkuhan]
to cheat on ... (commit adultery)	berselingkuh dari ...	[bərseliŋkuh dari ...]
jealous (adj)	cemburu	[tʃemburu]
to be jealous	cemburu	[tʃemburu]
divorce	perceraian	[pərtʃerajan]
to divorce (vi)	bercerai	[bərtʃeraj]
to quarrel (vi)	bertengkar	[bərteŋkar]
to be reconciled (after an argument)	berdamai	[bərdamaj]
together (adv)	bersama	[bərsama]
sex	seks	[seks]
happiness	kebahagiaan	[kebahagia'an]
happy (adj)	berbahagia	[bərbahagia]
misfortune (accident)	kemalangan	[kemalaŋan]
unhappy (adj)	malang	[malaŋ]

Character. Feelings. Emotions

58. Feelings. Emotions

feeling (emotion)	**perasaan**	[pərasa'an]
feelings	**perasaan**	[pərasa'an]
to feel (vt)	**merasa**	[merasa]
hunger	**kelaparan**	[kelaparan]
to be hungry	**lapar**	[lapar]
thirst	**kehausan**	[kehausan]
to be thirsty	**haus**	[haus]
sleepiness	**kantuk**	[kantu']
to feel sleepy	**mengantuk**	[məŋantu']
tiredness	**rasa lelah**	[rasa lelah]
tired (adj)	**lelah**	[lelah]
to get tired	**lelah**	[lelah]
mood (humour)	**suasana hati**	[suasana hati]
boredom	**kebosanan**	[kebosanan]
to be bored	**bosan**	[bosan]
seclusion	**kesendirian**	[kesendirian]
to seclude oneself	**menyendiri**	[mənjendiri]
to worry (make anxious)	**membuat khawatir**	[membuat hawatir]
to be worried	**khawatir**	[hawatir]
worrying (n)	**kekhawatiran**	[kehawatiran]
anxiety	**kegelisahan**	[kegelisahan]
preoccupied (adj)	**prihatin**	[prihatin]
to be nervous	**gugup, gelisah**	[gugup], [gelisah]
to panic (vi)	**panik**	[pani']
hope	**harapan**	[harapan]
to hope (vi, vt)	**berharap**	[bərharap]
certainty	**kepastian**	[kepastian]
certain, sure (adj)	**pasti**	[pasti]
uncertainty	**ketidakpastian**	[ketidakpastian]
uncertain (adj)	**tidak pasti**	[tida' pasti]
drunk (adj)	**mabuk**	[mabu']
sober (adj)	**sadar, tidak mabuk**	[sadar], [tida' mabu']
weak (adj)	**lemah**	[lemah]
happy (adj)	**berbahagia**	[bərbahagia]
to scare (vt)	**menakuti**	[mənakuti]
fury (madness)	**kemarahan**	[kemarahan]
rage (fury)	**kemarahan**	[kemarahan]
depression	**depresi**	[depresi]
discomfort (unease)	**ketidaknyamanan**	[ketidaknjamanan]

comfort	kenyamanan	[kenjamanan]
to regret (be sorry)	menyesal	[mənjesal]
regret	penyesalan	[penjesalan]
bad luck	kesialan	[kesialan]
sadness	kekesalan	[kekesalan]

shame (remorse)	rasa malu	[rasa malu]
gladness	kegirangan	[kegiraŋan]
enthusiasm, zeal	antusiasme	[antusiasme]
enthusiast	antusias	[antusias]
to show enthusiasm	memperlihatkan antusiasme	[memperlihatkan antusiasme]

59. Character. Personality

character	watak	[wata⁷]
character flaw	kepincangan	[kepintʃaŋan]
mind	otak	[ota⁷]
reason	akal	[akal]

conscience	nurani	[nurani]
habit (custom)	kebiasaan	[kebiasa'an]
ability (talent)	kemampuan, bakat	[kemampuan], [bakat]
can (e.g. ~ swim)	dapat	[dapat]

patient (adj)	sabar	[sabar]
impatient (adj)	tidak sabar	[tida' sabar]
curious (inquisitive)	ingin tahu	[iŋin tahu]
curiosity	rasa ingin tahu	[rasa iŋin tahu]

modesty	kerendahan hati	[kerendahan hati]
modest (adj)	rendah hati	[rendah hati]
immodest (adj)	tidak tahu malu	[tida' tahu malu]

laziness	kemalasan	[kemalasan]
lazy (adj)	malas	[malas]
lazy person (masc.)	pemalas	[pemalas]

cunning (n)	kelicikan	[kelitʃikan]
cunning (as adj)	licik	[litʃi⁷]
distrust	ketidakpercayaan	[ketidakpertʃaja'an]
distrustful (adj)	tidak percaya	[tida' pertʃaja]

generosity	kemurahan hati	[kemurahan hati]
generous (adj)	murah hati	[murah hati]
talented (adj)	berbakat	[bərbakat]
talent	bakat	[bakat]

courageous (adj)	berani	[bərani]
courage	keberanian	[keberanian]
honest (adj)	jujur	[dʒ'udʒ'ur]
honesty	kejujuran	[kedʒ'udʒ'uran]
careful (cautious)	berhati-hati	[bərhati-hati]
brave (courageous)	berani	[bərani]

serious (adj)	serius	[serius]
strict (severe, stern)	keras	[keras]
decisive (adj)	tegas	[tegas]
indecisive (adj)	ragu-ragu	[ragu-ragu]
shy, timid (adj)	malu	[malu]
shyness, timidity	sifat pemalu	[sifat pemalu]
confidence (trust)	kepercayaan	[kepertʃaja'an]
to believe (trust)	percaya	[pərtʃaja]
trusting (credulous)	mudah percaya	[mudah pərtʃaja]
sincerely (adv)	ikhlas	[ihlas]
sincere (adj)	ikhlas	[ihlas]
sincerity	keikhlasan	[keihlasan]
open (person)	terbuka	[tərbuka]
calm (adj)	tenang	[tenaŋ]
frank (sincere)	terus terang	[terus teraŋ]
naïve (adj)	naif	[naif]
absent-minded (adj)	lalai	[lalaj]
funny (odd)	lucu	[lutʃu]
greed, stinginess	kerakusan	[kerakusan]
greedy, stingy (adj)	rakus	[rakus]
stingy (adj)	pelit, kikir	[pelit], [kikir]
evil (adj)	jahat	[dʒɪahat]
stubborn (adj)	keras kepala, degil	[keras kepala], [degil]
unpleasant (adj)	tidak menyenangkan	[tida' menjenaŋkan]
selfish person (masc.)	egois	[egois]
selfish (adj)	egoistis	[egoistis]
coward	penakut	[penakut]
cowardly (adj)	penakut	[penakut]

60. Sleep. Dreams

to sleep (vi)	tidur	[tidur]
sleep, sleeping	tidur	[tidur]
dream	mimpi	[mimpi]
to dream (in sleep)	bermimpi	[bərmimpi]
sleepy (adj)	mengantuk	[məŋantu']
bed	ranjang	[randʒɪaŋ]
mattress	kasur	[kasur]
blanket (eiderdown)	selimut	[selimut]
pillow	bantal	[bantal]
sheet	seprai	[sepraj]
insomnia	insomnia	[insomnia]
sleepless (adj)	tanpa tidur	[tanpa tidur]
sleeping pill	obat tidur	[obat tidur]
to take a sleeping pill	meminum obat tidur	[meminum obat tidur]
to feel sleepy	mengantuk	[məŋantu']

to yawn (vi)	menguap	[məɳuap]
to go to bed	tidur	[tidur]
to make up the bed	menyiapkan ranjang	[mənjiapkan randʒ'aɳ]
to fall asleep	tertidur	[tərtidur]

nightmare	mimpi buruk	[mimpi buru']
snore, snoring	dengkuran	[deɳkuran]
to snore (vi)	berdengkur	[bərdeɳkur]

alarm clock	weker	[weker]
to wake (vt)	membangunkan	[membaɳunkan]
to wake up	bangun	[baɳun]
to get up (vi)	bangun	[baɳun]
to have a wash	mencuci muka	[məntʃutʃi muka]

61. Humour. Laughter. Gladness

humour (wit, fun)	humor	[humor]
sense of humour	rasa humor	[rasa humor]
to enjoy oneself	bersukaria	[bərsukaria]
cheerful (merry)	riang, gembira	[riaɳ], [gembira]
merriment (gaiety)	keriangan, kegembiraan	[keriaɳan], [kegembira'an]

smile	senyuman	[senyuman]
to smile (vi)	tersenyum	[tərsenyum]
to start laughing	tertawa	[tərtawa]
to laugh (vi)	tertawa	[tərtawa]
laugh, laughter	gelak tawa	[gela' tawa]

anecdote	anekdot, lelucon	[anekdot], [lelutʃon]
funny (anecdote, etc.)	lucu	[lutʃu]
funny (odd)	lucu	[lutʃu]

to joke (vi)	bergurau	[bərgurau]
joke (verbal)	lelucon	[lelutʃon]
joy (emotion)	kegembiraan	[kegembira'an]
to rejoice (vi)	bergembira	[bərgembira]
joyful (adj)	gembira	[gembira]

62. Discussion, conversation. Part 1

| communication | komunikasi | [komunikasi] |
| to communicate | berkomunikasi | [bərkomunikasi] |

conversation	pembicaraan	[pembitʃara'an]
dialogue	dialog	[dialog]
discussion (discourse)	diskusi	[diskusi]
dispute (debate)	perdebatan	[pərdebatan]
to dispute, to debate	berdebat	[bərdebat]

| interlocutor | lawan bicara | [lawan bitʃara] |
| topic (theme) | topik, tema | [topik], [tema] |

point of view	**sudut pandang**	[sudut pandaŋ]
opinion (point of view)	**opini, pendapat**	[opini], [pendapat]
speech (talk)	**pidato, tuturan**	[pidato], [tuturan]
discussion (of a report, etc.)	**pembicaraan**	[pembitʃaraʔan]
to discuss (vt)	**membicarakan**	[membitʃarakan]
talk (conversation)	**pembicaraan**	[pembitʃaraʔan]
to talk (to chat)	**berbicara**	[bərbitʃara]
meeting (encounter)	**pertemuan**	[pərtemuan]
to meet (vi, vt)	**bertemu**	[bərtemu]
proverb	**peribahasa**	[pəribahasa]
saying	**peribahasa**	[pəribahasa]
riddle (poser)	**teka-teki**	[teka-teki]
to pose a riddle	**memberi teka-teki**	[memberi teka-teki]
password	**kata sandi**	[kata sandi]
secret	**rahasia**	[rahasia]
oath (vow)	**sumpah**	[sumpah]
to swear (an oath)	**bersumpah**	[bərsumpah]
promise	**janji**	[dʒˈandʒi]
to promise (vt)	**berjanji**	[bərdʒˈandʒi]
advice (counsel)	**nasihat**	[nasihat]
to advise (vt)	**menasihati**	[mənasihati]
to follow one's advice	**mengikuti nasihat**	[məŋikuti nasihat]
to listen to … (obey)	**mendengar …**	[məndeŋar …]
news	**berita**	[berita]
sensation (news)	**sensasi**	[sensasi]
information (report)	**data, informasi**	[data], [informasi]
conclusion (decision)	**kesimpulan**	[kesimpulan]
voice	**suara**	[suara]
compliment	**pujian**	[pudʒian]
kind (nice)	**ramah**	[ramah]
word	**kata**	[kata]
phrase	**frasa**	[frasa]
answer	**jawaban**	[dʒˈawaban]
truth	**kebenaran**	[kebenaran]
lie	**kebohongan**	[kebohoŋan]
thought	**pikiran**	[pikiran]
idea (inspiration)	**ide**	[ide]
fantasy	**fantasi**	[fantasi]

63. Discussion, conversation. Part 2

respected (adj)	**terhormat**	[tərhormat]
to respect (vt)	**menghormati**	[məŋhormati]
respect	**penghormatan**	[peŋhormatan]
Dear … (letter)	**Yth. … (Yang Terhormat)**	[yaŋ tərhormat]
to introduce (sb to sb)	**memperkenalkan**	[memperkenalkan]

to make acquaintance	berkenalan	[bərkenalan]
intention	niat	[niat]
to intend (have in mind)	berniat	[bərniat]
wish	pengharapan	[peŋharapan]
to wish (~ good luck)	mengharapkan	[məŋharapkan]

surprise (astonishment)	keheranan	[keheranan]
to surprise (amaze)	mengherankan	[məŋherankan]
to be surprised	heran	[heran]

to give (vt)	memberi	[memberi]
to take (get hold of)	mengambil	[məŋambil]
to give back	mengembalikan	[məŋembalikan]
to return (give back)	mengembalikan	[məŋembalikan]

to apologize (vi)	meminta maaf	[meminta maʔaf]
apology	permintaan maaf	[pərmintaʔan maʔaf]
to forgive (vt)	memaafkan	[memaʔafkan]

to talk (speak)	berbicara	[bərbitʃara]
to listen (vi)	mendengarkan	[məndeŋarkan]
to hear out	mendengar	[məndeŋar]
to understand (vt)	mengerti	[məŋerti]

to show (to display)	menunjukkan	[mənundʒｉuʔkan]
to look at ...	melihat ...	[melihat ...]
to call (yell for sb)	memanggil	[memaŋgil]
to distract (disturb)	mengganggu	[məŋgaŋgu]
to disturb (vt)	mengganggu	[məŋgaŋgu]
to pass (to hand sth)	menyampaikan	[mənjampajkan]

demand (request)	permintaan	[pərmintaʔan]
to request (ask)	meminta	[meminta]
demand (firm request)	tuntutan	[tuntutan]
to demand (request firmly)	menuntut	[mənuntut]

to tease (call names)	mengejek	[mənedʒｉeʔ]
to mock (make fun of)	mencemooh	[məntʃemooh]
mockery, derision	cemoohan	[tʃemoohan]
nickname	nama panggilan	[nama paŋgilan]

insinuation	isyarat	[iʃarat]
to insinuate (imply)	mengisyaratkan	[məŋiʃaratkan]
to mean (vt)	berarti	[bərarti]

description	penggambaran	[peŋgambaran]
to describe (vt)	menggambarkan	[məŋgambarkan]
praise (compliments)	pujian	[pudʒian]
to praise (vt)	memuji	[memudʒi]

disappointment	kekecewaan	[keketʃewaʔan]
to disappoint (vt)	mengecewakan	[məŋetʃewakan]
to be disappointed	kecewa	[ketʃewa]

supposition	dugaan	[dugaʔan]
to suppose (assume)	menduga	[mənduga]

| warning (caution) | peringatan | [pəriŋatan] |
| to warn (vt) | memperingatkan | [memperiŋatkan] |

64. Discussion, conversation. Part 3

| to talk into (convince) | meyakinkan | [meyakinkan] |
| to calm down (vt) | menenangkan | [mənenaŋkan] |

silence (~ is golden)	kebisuan	[kebisuan]
to be silent (not speaking)	membisu	[membisu]
to whisper (vi, vt)	berbisik	[bərbisiʔ]
whisper	bisikan	[bisikan]

| frankly, sincerely (adv) | terus terang | [terus təraŋ] |
| in my opinion ... | menurut saya ... | [mənurut saja ...] |

detail (of the story)	detail, perincian	[detajl], [pərintʃian]
detailed (adj)	mendetail	[məndetajl]
in detail (adv)	dengan mendetail	[deŋan mendetajl]

| hint, clue | petunjuk | [petundʒʲuʔ] |
| to give a hint | memberi petunjuk | [memberi petundʒʲuʔ] |

look (glance)	melihat	[melihat]
to have a look	melihat	[melihat]
fixed (look)	kaku	[kaku]
to blink (vi)	berkedip	[bərkedip]
to wink (vi)	mengedipkan mata	[məŋedipkan mata]
to nod (in assent)	mengangguk	[mənaŋguʔ]

sigh	desah	[desah]
to sigh (vi)	mendesah	[məndesah]
to shudder (vi)	tersentak	[tərsentaʔ]
gesture	gerak tangan	[geraʔ taŋan]
to touch (one's arm, etc.)	menyentuh	[mənjentuh]
to seize (e.g., ~ by the arm)	memegang	[memegaŋ]
to tap (on the shoulder)	menepuk	[mənepuʔ]

Look out!	Awas! Hati-hati!	[awas!], [hati-hati!]
Really?	Sungguh?	[suŋguh?]
Are you sure?	Kamu yakin?	[kamu yakin?]
Good luck!	Semoga behasil!	[semoga behasil!]
I see!	Begitu!	[begitu!]
What a pity!	Sayang sekali!	[sajaŋ sekali!]

65. Agreement. Refusal

consent	persetujuan	[pərsetudʒʲuan]
to consent (vi)	setuju, ijin	[setudʒʲu], [idʒin]
approval	persetujuan	[pərsetudʒʲuan]
to approve (vt)	menyetujui	[mənjetudʒʲui]
refusal	penolakan	[penolakan]

to refuse (vi, vt)	menolak	[mənolaʔ]
Great!	Bagus!	[bagus!]
All right!	Baiklah! Baik!	[bajklah!], [bajʔ!]
Okay! (I agree)	Baiklah! Baik!	[bajklah!], [bajʔ!]

forbidden (adj)	larangan	[laraŋan]
it's forbidden	dilarang	[dilaraŋ]
it's impossible	mustahil	[mustahil]
incorrect (adj)	salah	[salah]

to reject (~ a demand)	menolak	[mənolaʔ]
to support (cause, idea)	mendukung	[məndukuŋ]
to accept (~ an apology)	menerima	[mənerima]

to confirm (vt)	mengonfirmasi	[məŋonfirmasi]
confirmation	konfirmasi	[konfirmasi]
permission	izin	[izin]
to permit (vt)	mengizinkan	[məŋizinkan]
decision	keputusan	[keputusan]
to say nothing (hold one's tongue)	membisu	[membisu]

condition (term)	syarat	[ʃarat]
excuse (pretext)	alasan, dalih	[alasan], [dalih]
praise (compliments)	pujian	[pudʒian]
to praise (vt)	memuji	[memudʒi]

66. Success. Good luck. Failure

success	sukses, berhasil	[sukses], [bərhasil]
successfully (adv)	dengan sukses	[deŋan sukses]
successful (adj)	sukses, berhasil	[sukses], [bərhasil]

luck (good luck)	keberuntungan	[keberuntuŋan]
Good luck!	Semoga behasil!	[semoga behasil!]
lucky (e.g. ~ day)	beruntung	[bəruntuŋ]
lucky (fortunate)	beruntung	[bəruntuŋ]

failure	kegagalan	[kegagalan]
misfortune	kesialan	[kesialan]
bad luck	kesialan	[kesialan]
unsuccessful (adj)	gagal	[gagal]
catastrophe	gagal total	[gagal total]

pride	kebanggaan	[kebaŋaʔan]
proud (adj)	bangga	[baŋga]
to be proud	bangga	[baŋga]

winner	pemenang	[pemenaŋ]
to win (vi)	menang	[menaŋ]
to lose (not win)	kalah	[kalah]
try	percobaan	[pərtʃobaʔan]
to try (vi)	mencoba	[məntʃoba]
chance (opportunity)	kans, peluang	[kans], [peluaŋ]

67. Quarrels. Negative emotions

shout (scream)	teriakan	[təriakan]
to shout (vi)	berteriak	[bərteria']
to start to cry out	berteriak	[bərteria']
quarrel	pertengkaran	[pərteŋkaran]
to quarrel (vi)	bertengkar	[bərteŋkar]
fight (squabble)	pertengkaran	[pərteŋkaran]
to make a scene	bertengkar	[bərteŋkar]
conflict	konflik	[konfli']
misunderstanding	kesalahpahaman	[kesalahpahaman]
insult	penghinaan	[pəŋhina'an]
to insult (vt)	menghina	[məŋhina]
insulted (adj)	terhina	[tərhina]
resentment	perasaan tersinggung	[pərasa'an tərsiŋguŋ]
to offend (vt)	menyinggung	[məɲjiŋguŋ]
to take offence	tersinggung	[tərsiŋguŋ]
indignation	kemarahan	[kemarahan]
to be indignant	marah	[marah]
complaint	komplain, pengaduan	[kompleyn], [pəɲaduan]
to complain (vi, vt)	mengeluh	[məŋeluh]
apology	permintaan maaf	[pərminta'an ma'af]
to apologize (vi)	meminta maaf	[meminta ma'af]
to beg pardon	minta maaf	[minta ma'af]
criticism	kritik	[kriti']
to criticize (vt)	mengkritik	[məŋkriti']
accusation (charge)	tuduhan	[tuduhan]
to accuse (vt)	menuduh	[mənuduh]
revenge	dendam	[dendam]
to avenge (get revenge)	membalas dendam	[membalas dendam]
to pay back	membalas	[membalas]
disdain	penghinaan	[pəŋhina'an]
to despise (vt)	benci, membenci	[bentʃi], [membentʃi]
hatred, hate	rasa benci	[rasa bentʃi]
to hate (vt)	membenci	[membentʃi]
nervous (adj)	gugup, grogi	[gugup], [grogi]
to be nervous	gugup, gelisah	[gugup], [gelisah]
angry (mad)	marah	[marah]
to make angry	membuat marah	[membuat marah]
humiliation	penghinaan	[pəŋhina'an]
to humiliate (vt)	merendahkan	[merendahkan]
to humiliate oneself	merendahkan diri sendiri	[merendahkan diri sendiri]
shock	keterkejutan	[keterkedʒutan]
to shock (vt)	mengejutkan	[məŋedʒutkan]
trouble (e.g. serious ~)	kesulitan	[kesulitan]

unpleasant (adj)	**tidak menyenangkan**	[tida' menjenaŋkan]
fear (dread)	**ketakutan**	[ketakutan]
terrible (storm, heat)	**dahsyat**	[dahʃat]
scary (e.g. ~ story)	**menakutkan**	[mənakutkan]
horror	**horor, ketakutan**	[horor], [ketakutan]
awful (crime, news)	**buruk, parah**	[buruk], [parah]
to begin to tremble	**gemetar**	[gemetar]
to cry (weep)	**menangis**	[mənaŋis]
to start crying	**menangis**	[mənaŋis]
tear	**air mata**	[air mata]
fault	**kesalahan**	[kesalahan]
guilt (feeling)	**rasa bersalah**	[rasa bərsalah]
dishonor (disgrace)	**aib**	[aib]
protest	**protes**	[protes]
stress	**stres**	[stres]
to disturb (vt)	**mengganggu**	[məŋgaŋgu]
to be furious	**marah**	[marah]
angry (adj)	**marah**	[marah]
to end (~ a relationship)	**menghentikan**	[mənhentikan]
to swear (at sb)	**menyumpahi**	[mənyumpahi]
to scare (become afraid)	**takut**	[takut]
to hit (strike with hand)	**memukul**	[memukul]
to fight (street fight, etc.)	**berkelahi**	[bərkelahi]
to settle (a conflict)	**menyelesaikan**	[mənjelesajkan]
discontented (adj)	**tidak puas**	[tida' puas]
furious (adj)	**garam**	[garam]
It's not good!	**Tidak baik!**	[tida' bai'!]
It's bad!	**Jelek! Buruk!**	[dʒ'ele'!], [buru'!]

Medicine

68. Diseases

illness	**penyakit**	[penjakit]
to be ill	**sakit**	[sakit]
health	**kesehatan**	[kesehatan]
runny nose (coryza)	**hidung meler**	[hiduŋ meler]
tonsillitis	**radang tonsil**	[radaŋ tonsil]
cold (illness)	**pilek, selesma**	[pilek], [selesma]
to catch a cold	**masuk angin**	[masuʔ aŋin]
bronchitis	**bronkitis**	[bronkitis]
pneumonia	**radang paru-paru**	[radaŋ paru-paru]
flu, influenza	**flu**	[flu]
shortsighted (adj)	**rabun jauh**	[rabun dʒ'auh]
longsighted (adj)	**rabun dekat**	[rabun dekat]
strabismus (crossed eyes)	**mata juling**	[mata dʒ'uliŋ]
squint-eyed (adj)	**bermata juling**	[bərmata dʒ'uliŋ]
cataract	**katarak**	[kataraʔ]
glaucoma	**glaukoma**	[glaukoma]
stroke	**stroke**	[stroke]
heart attack	**infark**	[infarʔ]
myocardial infarction	**serangan jantung**	[seraŋan dʒ'antuŋ]
paralysis	**kelumpuhan**	[kelumpuhan]
to paralyse (vt)	**melumpuhkan**	[melumpuhkan]
allergy	**alergi**	[alergi]
asthma	**asma**	[asma]
diabetes	**diabetes**	[diabetes]
toothache	**sakit gigi**	[sakit gigi]
caries	**karies**	[karies]
diarrhoea	**diare**	[diare]
constipation	**konstipasi, sembelit**	[konstipasi], [sembelit]
stomach upset	**gangguan pencernaan**	[gaŋuan pentʃarnaʔan]
food poisoning	**keracunan makanan**	[keratʃunan makanan]
to get food poisoning	**keracunan makanan**	[keratʃunan makanan]
arthritis	**artritis**	[artritis]
rickets	**rakitis**	[rakitis]
rheumatism	**rematik**	[rematiʔ]
atherosclerosis	**aterosklerosis**	[aterosklerosis]
gastritis	**radang perut**	[radaŋ pərut]
appendicitis	**apendisitis**	[apendisitis]

cholecystitis	**radang pundi empedu**	[radaŋ pundi empedu]
ulcer	**tukak lambung**	[tuka' lambuŋ]
measles	**penyakit campak**	[penjakit t͡ʃampa']
rubella (German measles)	**penyakit campak Jerman**	[penjakit t͡ʃampa' d͡ʒʲerman]
jaundice	**sakit kuning**	[sakit kuniŋ]
hepatitis	**hepatitis**	[hepatitis]
schizophrenia	**skizofrenia**	[skizofrenia]
rabies (hydrophobia)	**rabies**	[rabies]
neurosis	**neurosis**	[neurosis]
concussion	**gegar otak**	[gegar ota']
cancer	**kanker**	[kanker]
sclerosis	**sklerosis**	[sklerosis]
multiple sclerosis	**sklerosis multipel**	[sklerosis multipel]
alcoholism	**alkoholisme**	[alkoholisme]
alcoholic (n)	**alkoholik**	[alkoholi']
syphilis	**sifilis**	[sifilis]
AIDS	**AIDS**	[ajds]
tumour	**tumor**	[tumor]
malignant (adj)	**ganas**	[ganas]
benign (adj)	**jinak**	[d͡ʒina']
fever	**demam**	[demam]
malaria	**malaria**	[malaria]
gangrene	**gangren**	[gaŋren]
seasickness	**mabuk laut**	[mabu' laut]
epilepsy	**epilepsi**	[epilepsi]
epidemic	**epidemi**	[epidemi]
typhus	**tifus**	[tifus]
tuberculosis	**tuberkulosis**	[tuberkulosis]
cholera	**kolera**	[kolera]
plague (bubonic ~)	**penyakit pes**	[penjakit pes]

69. Symptoms. Treatments. Part 1

symptom	**gejala**	[ged͡ʒʲala]
temperature	**temperatur, suhu**	[temperatur], [suhu]
high temperature (fever)	**temperatur tinggi**	[temperatur tiŋgi]
pulse (heartbeat)	**denyut nadi**	[denyut nadi]
dizziness (vertigo)	**rasa pening**	[rasa peniŋ]
hot (adj)	**panas**	[panas]
shivering	**menggigil**	[məŋgigil]
pale (e.g. ~ face)	**pucat**	[put͡ʃat]
cough	**batuk**	[batu']
to cough (vi)	**batuk**	[batu']
to sneeze (vi)	**bersin**	[bersin]
faint	**pingsan**	[piŋsan]

to faint (vi)	jatuh pingsan	[dʒ'atuh piŋsan]
bruise (hématome)	luka memar	[luka memar]
bump (lump)	bengkak	[beŋka']
to bang (bump)	terantuk	[tərantu']
contusion (bruise)	luka memar	[luka memar]
to get a bruise	kena luka memar	[kena luka memar]
to limp (vi)	pincang	[pintʃaŋ]
dislocation	keseleo	[keseleo]
to dislocate (vt)	keseleo	[keseleo]
fracture	fraktura, patah tulang	[fraktura], [patah tulaŋ]
to have a fracture	patah tulang	[patah tulaŋ]
cut (e.g. paper ~)	teriris	[təriris]
to cut oneself	teriris	[təriris]
bleeding	perdarahan	[pərdarahan]
burn (injury)	luka bakar	[luka bakar]
to get burned	menderita luka bakar	[mənderita luka bakar]
to prick (vt)	menusuk	[mənusu']
to prick oneself	tertusuk	[tərtusu']
to injure (vt)	melukai	[melukaj]
injury	cedera	[tʃedera]
wound	luka	[luka]
trauma	trauma	[trauma]
to be delirious	mengigau	[məŋigau]
to stutter (vi)	gagap	[gagap]
sunstroke	sengatan matahari	[seŋatan matahari]

70. Symptoms. Treatments. Part 2

pain, ache	sakit	[sakit]
splinter (in foot, etc.)	selumbar	[selumbar]
sweat (perspiration)	keringat	[keriŋat]
to sweat (perspire)	berkeringat	[bərkeriŋat]
vomiting	muntah	[muntah]
convulsions	kram	[kram]
pregnant (adj)	hamil	[hamil]
to be born	lahir	[lahir]
delivery, labour	persalinan	[pərsalinan]
to deliver (~ a baby)	melahirkan	[melahirkan]
abortion	aborsi	[aborsi]
breathing, respiration	pernapasan	[pərnapasan]
in-breath (inhalation)	tarikan napas	[tarikan napas]
out-breath (exhalation)	napas keluar	[napas keluar]
to exhale (breathe out)	mengembuskan napas	[məŋembuskan napas]
to inhale (vi)	menarik napas	[mənari' napas]
disabled person	penderita cacat	[penderita tʃatʃat]
cripple	penderita cacat	[penderita tʃatʃat]

drug addict	pecandu narkoba	[petʃandu narkoba]
deaf (adj)	tunarungu	[tunaruŋu]
mute (adj)	tunawicara	[tunawitʃara]
deaf mute (adj)	tunarungu-wicara	[tunaruŋu-witʃara]

mad, insane (adj)	gila	[gila]
madman	lelaki gila	[lelaki gila]
(demented person)		
madwoman	perempuan gila	[pərempuan gila]
to go insane	menggila	[məŋgila]

gene	gen	[gen]
immunity	imunitas	[imunitas]
hereditary (adj)	turun-temurun	[turun-temurun]
congenital (adj)	bawaan	[bawa'an]

virus	virus	[virus]
microbe	mikroba	[mikroba]
bacterium	bakteri	[bakteri]
infection	infeksi	[infeksi]

71. Symptoms. Treatments. Part 3

| hospital | rumah sakit | [rumah sakit] |
| patient | pasien | [pasien] |

diagnosis	diagnosis	[diagnosis]
cure	perawatan	[pərawatan]
medical treatment	pengobatan medis	[pəŋobatan medis]
to get treatment	berobat	[bərobat]
to treat (~ a patient)	merawat	[merawat]
to nurse (look after)	merawat	[merawat]
care (nursing ~)	pengasuhan	[pəɲasuhan]

operation, surgery	operasi, pembedahan	[operasi], [pembedahan]
to bandage (head, limb)	membalut	[membalut]
bandaging	pembalutan	[pembalutan]

vaccination	vaksinasi	[vaksinasi]
to vaccinate (vt)	memvaksinasi	[memvaksinasi]
injection	suntikan	[suntikan]
to give an injection	menyuntik	[məɲunti']

attack	serangan	[seraŋan]
amputation	amputasi	[amputasi]
to amputate (vt)	mengamputasi	[məɲamputasi]
coma	koma	[koma]
to be in a coma	dalam keadaan koma	[dalam keada'an koma]
intensive care	perawatan intensif	[pərawatan intensif]

to recover (~ from flu)	sembuh	[sembuh]
condition (patient's ~)	keadaan	[keada'an]
consciousness	kesadaran	[kesadaran]
memory (faculty)	memori, daya ingat	[memori], [daja iŋat]

to pull out (tooth)	mencabut	[mentʃabut]
filling	tambalan	[tambalan]
to fill (a tooth)	menambal	[mənambal]

| hypnosis | hipnosis | [hipnosis] |
| to hypnotize (vt) | menghipnosis | [məŋhipnosis] |

72. Doctors

doctor	dokter	[dokter]
nurse	suster, juru rawat	[suster], [dʒʲuru rawat]
personal doctor	dokter pribadi	[dokter pribadi]

dentist	dokter gigi	[dokter gigi]
optician	dokter mata	[dokter mata]
general practitioner	ahli penyakit dalam	[ahli penjakit dalam]
surgeon	dokter bedah	[dokter bedah]

psychiatrist	psikiater	[psikiater]
paediatrician	dokter anak	[dokter anaʔ]
psychologist	psikolog	[psikolog]
gynaecologist	ginekolog	[ginekolog]
cardiologist	kardiolog	[kardiolog]

73. Medicine. Drugs. Accessories

medicine, drug	obat	[obat]
remedy	obat	[obat]
to prescribe (vt)	meresepkan	[meresepkan]
prescription	resep	[resep]

tablet, pill	pil, tablet	[pil], [tablet]
ointment	salep	[salep]
ampoule	ampul	[ampul]
mixture, solution	obat cair	[obat tʃajr]
syrup	sirop	[sirop]
capsule	pil	[pil]
powder	bubuk	[bubuʔ]

gauze bandage	perban	[perban]
cotton wool	kapas	[kapas]
iodine	iodium	[iodium]

plaster	plester obat	[plester obat]
eyedropper	tetes mata	[tetes mata]
thermometer	termometer	[termometer]
syringe	alat suntik	[alat suntiʔ]

wheelchair	kursi roda	[kursi roda]
crutches	kruk	[kruʔ]
painkiller	obat bius	[obat bius]
laxative	laksatif, obat pencuci perut	[laksatif], [obat pentʃutʃi perut]

spirits (ethanol)	spiritus, alkohol	[spiritus], [alkohol]
medicinal herbs	tanaman obat	[tanaman obat]
herbal (~ tea)	herbal	[herbal]

74. Smoking. Tobacco products

tobacco	tembakau	[tembakau]
cigarette	rokok	[roko']
cigar	cerutu	[ʧerutu]
pipe	pipa	[pipa]
packet (of cigarettes)	bungkus	[buŋkus]

matches	korek api	[kore' api]
matchbox	kotak korek api	[kota' kore' api]
lighter	pemantik	[pemanti']
ashtray	asbak	[asba']
cigarette case	selepa	[selepa]

| cigarette holder | pemegang rokok | [pemegaŋ roko'] |
| filter (cigarette tip) | filter | [filter] |

to smoke (vi, vt)	merokok	[meroko']
to light a cigarette	menyulut rokok	[menyulut roko']
smoking	merokok	[meroko']
smoker	perokok	[peroko']

cigarette end	puntung rokok	[puntuŋ roko']
smoke, fumes	asap	[asap]
ash	abu	[abu]

HUMAN HABITAT

City

city, town	**kota**	[kota]
capital city	**ibu kota**	[ibu kota]
village	**desa**	[desa]
city map	**peta kota**	[peta kota]
city centre	**pusat kota**	[pusat kota]
suburb	**pinggir kota**	[piŋgir kota]
suburban (adj)	**pinggir kota**	[piŋgir kota]
outskirts	**pinggir**	[piŋgir]
environs (suburbs)	**daerah sekitarnya**	[daerah sekitarnja]
city block	**blok**	[blo']
residential block (area)	**blok perumahan**	[blo' pərumahan]
traffic	**lalu lintas**	[lalu lintas]
traffic lights	**lampu lalu lintas**	[lampu lalu lintas]
public transport	**angkot**	[aŋkot]
crossroads	**persimpangan**	[pərsimpaŋan]
zebra crossing	**penyeberangan**	[penjeberaŋan]
pedestrian subway	**terowongan penyeberangan**	[tərowoŋan penjeberaŋan]
to cross (~ the street)	**menyeberang**	[mənjeberaŋ]
pedestrian	**pejalan kaki**	[pedʒʲalan kaki]
pavement	**trotoar**	[trotoar]
bridge	**jembatan**	[dʒʲembatan]
embankment (river walk)	**tepi sungai**	[tepi suŋaj]
fountain	**air mancur**	[air mantʃur]
allée (garden walkway)	**jalan kecil**	[dʒʲalan ketʃil]
park	**taman**	[taman]
boulevard	**bulevar, adimarga**	[bulevar], [adimarga]
square	**lapangan**	[lapaŋan]
avenue (wide street)	**jalan raya**	[dʒʲalan raja]
street	**jalan**	[dʒʲalan]
side street	**gang**	[gaŋ]
dead end	**jalan buntu**	[dʒʲalan buntu]
house	**rumah**	[rumah]
building	**gedung**	[geduŋ]
skyscraper	**pencakar langit**	[pentʃakar laŋit]
facade	**bagian depan**	[bagian depan]

roof	atap	[atap]
window	jendela	[dʒʲendela]
arch	lengkungan	[leŋkuŋan]
column	pilar	[pilar]
corner	sudut	[sudut]

shop window	etalase	[etalase]
signboard (store sign, etc.)	papan nama	[papan nama]
poster (e.g., playbill)	poster	[poster]
advertising poster	poster iklan	[poster iklan]
hoarding	papan iklan	[papan iklan]

rubbish	sampah	[sampah]
rubbish bin	tong sampah	[toŋ sampah]
to litter (vi)	menyampah	[mənjampah]
rubbish dump	tempat pemrosesan akhir (TPA)	[tempat pemrosesan ahir]

telephone box	gardu telepon umum	[gardu telepon umum]
lamppost	tiang lampu	[tiaŋ lampu]
bench (park ~)	bangku	[baŋku]

police officer	polisi	[polisi]
police	polisi, kepolisian	[polisi], [kepolisian]
beggar	pengemis	[peɲemis]
homeless (n)	tuna wisma	[tuna wisma]

76. Urban institutions

shop	toko	[toko]
chemist, pharmacy	apotek, toko obat	[apotek], [toko obat]
optician (spectacles shop)	optik	[optiʔ]
shopping centre	toserba	[toserba]
supermarket	pasar swalayan	[pasar swalajan]

bakery	toko roti	[toko roti]
baker	pembuat roti	[pembuat roti]
cake shop	toko kue	[toko kue]
grocery shop	toko pangan	[toko paŋan]
butcher shop	toko daging	[toko dagiŋ]

| greengrocer | toko sayur | [toko sajur] |
| market | pasar | [pasar] |

coffee bar	warung kopi	[waruŋ kopi]
restaurant	restoran	[restoran]
pub, bar	kedai bir	[kedaj bir]
pizzeria	kedai piza	[kedaj piza]

hairdresser	salon rambut	[salon rambut]
post office	kantor pos	[kantor pos]
dry cleaners	penatu kimia	[penatu kimia]
photo studio	studio foto	[studio foto]
shoe shop	toko sepatu	[toko sepatu]

bookshop	**toko buku**	[toko buku]
sports shop	**toko alat olahraga**	[toko alat olahraga]
clothes repair shop	**reparasi pakaian**	[reparasi pakajan]
formal wear hire	**rental pakaian**	[rental pakajan]
video rental shop	**rental film**	[rental film]
circus	**sirkus**	[sirkus]
zoo	**kebun binatang**	[kebun binataŋ]
cinema	**bioskop**	[bioskop]
museum	**museum**	[museum]
library	**perpustakaan**	[pərpustaka'an]
theatre	**teater**	[teater]
opera (opera house)	**opera**	[opera]
nightclub	**klub malam**	[klub malam]
casino	**kasino**	[kasino]
mosque	**masjid**	[masdʒid]
synagogue	**sinagoga, kanisah**	[sinagoga], [kanisah]
cathedral	**katedral**	[katedral]
temple	**kuil, candi**	[kuil], [tʃandi]
church	**gereja**	[geredʒʲa]
college	**institut, perguruan tinggi**	[institut], [pərguruan tiŋgi]
university	**universitas**	[universitas]
school	**sekolah**	[sekolah]
prefecture	**prefektur, distrik**	[prefektur], [distri']
town hall	**balai kota**	[balaj kota]
hotel	**hotel**	[hotel]
bank	**bank**	[ban']
embassy	**kedutaan besar**	[keduta'an besar]
travel agency	**kantor pariwisata**	[kantor pariwisata]
information office	**kantor penerangan**	[kantor peneraŋan]
currency exchange	**kantor penukaran uang**	[kantor penukaran uaŋ]
underground, tube	**kereta api bawah tanah**	[kereta api bawah tanah]
hospital	**rumah sakit**	[rumah sakit]
petrol station	**SPBU, stasiun bensin**	[es-pe-be-u], [stasjun bensin]
car park	**tempat parkir**	[tempat parkir]

77. Urban transport

bus, coach	**bus**	[bus]
tram	**trem**	[trem]
trolleybus	**bus listrik**	[bus listri']
route (bus ~)	**trayek**	[trae']
number (e.g. bus ~)	**nomor**	[nomor]
to go by ...	**naik ...**	[nai' ...]
to get on (~ the bus)	**naik**	[nai']

to get off ...	turun ...	[turun ...]
stop (e.g. bus ~)	halte, pemberhentian	[halte], [pemberhentian]
next stop	halte berikutnya	[halte bərikutnja]
terminus	halte terakhir	[halte tərahir]
timetable	jadwal	[dʒ'adwal]
to wait (vt)	menunggu	[mənuŋgu]
ticket	tiket	[tiket]
fare	harga karcis	[harga kartʃis]
cashier (ticket seller)	kasir	[kasir]
ticket inspection	pemeriksaan tiket	[pemeriksa'an tiket]
ticket inspector	kondektur	[kondektur]
to be late (for ...)	terlambat ...	[tərlambat ...]
to miss (~ the train, etc.)	ketinggalan	[ketiŋgalan]
to be in a hurry	tergesa-gesa	[tərgesa-gesa]
taxi, cab	taksi	[taksi]
taxi driver	sopir taksi	[sopir taksi]
by taxi	naik taksi	[nai' taksi]
taxi rank	pangkalan taksi	[paŋkalan taksi]
to call a taxi	memanggil taksi	[memaŋgil taksi]
to take a taxi	menaiki taksi	[mənajki taksi]
traffic	lalu lintas	[lalu lintas]
traffic jam	kemacetan lalu lintas	[kematʃetan lalu lintas]
rush hour	jam sibuk	[dʒ'am sibu']
to park (vi)	parkir	[parkir]
to park (vt)	memarkir	[memarkir]
car park	tempat parkir	[tempat parkir]
underground, tube	kereta api bawah tanah	[kereta api bawah tanah]
station	stasiun	[stasiun]
to take the tube	naik kereta api bawah tanah	[nai' kereta api bawah tanah]
train	kereta api	[kereta api]
train station	stasiun kereta api	[stasiun kereta api]

78. Sightseeing

monument	monumen, patung	[monumen], [patuŋ]
fortress	benteng	[benteŋ]
palace	istana	[istana]
castle	kastil	[kastil]
tower	menara	[mənara]
mausoleum	mausoleum	[mausoleum]
architecture	arsitektur	[arsitektur]
medieval (adj)	abad pertengahan	[abad pərteŋahan]
ancient (adj)	kuno	[kuno]
national (adj)	nasional	[nasional]
famous (monument, etc.)	terkenal	[tərkenal]
tourist	turis, wisatawan	[turis], [wisatawan]

guide (person)	pemandu wisata	[pemandu wisata]
excursion, sightseeing tour	ekskursi	[ekskursi]
to show (vt)	menunjukkan	[mənundʒiuʾkan]
to tell (vt)	menceritakan	[məntʃeritakan]

to find (vt)	mendapatkan	[məndapatkan]
to get lost (lose one's way)	tersesat	[tərsesat]
map (e.g. underground ~)	denah	[denah]
map (e.g. city ~)	peta	[peta]

souvenir, gift	suvenir	[suvenir]
gift shop	toko suvenir	[toko suvenir]
to take pictures	memotret	[memotret]
to have one's picture taken	berfoto	[bərfoto]

79. Shopping

to buy (purchase)	membeli	[membeli]
shopping	belanjaan	[belandʒia'an]
to go shopping	berbelanja	[bərbelandʒia]
shopping	berbelanja	[bərbelandʒia]

| to be open (ab. shop) | buka | [buka] |
| to be closed | tutup | [tutup] |

footwear, shoes	sepatu	[sepatu]
clothes, clothing	pakaian	[pakajan]
cosmetics	kosmetik	[kosmetiʾ]
food products	produk makanan	[produʾ makanan]
gift, present	hadiah	[hadiah]

| shop assistant (masc.) | pramuniaga | [pramuniaga] |
| shop assistant (fem.) | pramuniaga perempuan | [pramuniaga pərempuan] |

cash desk	kas	[kas]
mirror	cermin	[tʃermin]
counter (shop ~)	konter	[konter]
fitting room	kamar pas	[kamar pas]

to try on	mengepas	[məŋepas]
to fit (ab. dress, etc.)	pas, cocok	[pas], [tʃotʃoʾ]
to fancy (vt)	suka	[suka]

price	harga	[harga]
price tag	label harga	[label harga]
to cost (vt)	berharga	[bərharga]
How much?	Berapa?	[bərapa?]
discount	diskon	[diskon]

inexpensive (adj)	tidak mahal	[tidaʾ mahal]
cheap (adj)	murah	[murah]
expensive (adj)	mahal	[mahal]
It's expensive	Ini mahal	[ini mahal]
hire (n)	rental, persewaan	[rental], [pərsewa'an]

to hire (~ a dinner jacket)	menyewa	[mənjewa]
credit (trade credit)	kredit	[kredit]
on credit (adv)	secara kredit	[setʃara kredit]

80. Money

money	uang	[uaŋ]
currency exchange	pertukaran mata uang	[pərtukaran mata uaŋ]
exchange rate	nilai tukar	[nilaj tukar]
cashpoint	Anjungan Tunai Mandiri, ATM	[andʒ'uŋan tunaj mandiri], [a-te-em]
coin	koin	[koin]
dollar	dolar	[dolar]
euro	euro	[euro]
lira	lira	[lira]
Deutschmark	Mark Jerman	[mar' dʒ'erman]
franc	franc	[frantʃ]
pound sterling	poundsterling	[paundsterliŋ]
yen	yen	[yen]
debt	utang	[utaŋ]
debtor	pengutang	[peŋutaŋ]
to lend (money)	meminjamkan	[memindʒ'amkan]
to borrow (vi, vt)	meminjam	[memindʒ'am]
bank	bank	[ban']
account	rekening	[rekeniŋ]
to deposit (vt)	memasukkan	[memasu'kan]
to deposit into the account	memasukkan ke rekening	[memasu'kan ke rekeniŋ]
to withdraw (vt)	menarik uang	[mənari' uaŋ]
credit card	kartu kredit	[kartu kredit]
cash	uang kontan, uang tunai	[uaŋ kontan], [uaŋ tunaj]
cheque	cek	[tʃe']
to write a cheque	menulis cek	[mənulis tʃe']
chequebook	buku cek	[buku tʃe']
wallet	dompet	[dompet]
purse	dompet, pundi-pundi	[dompet], [pundi-pundi]
safe	brankas	[brankas]
heir	pewaris	[pewaris]
inheritance	warisan	[warisan]
fortune (wealth)	kekayaan	[kekaja'an]
lease	sewa	[sewa]
rent (money)	uang sewa	[uaŋ sewa]
to rent (sth from sb)	menyewa	[mənjewa]
price	harga	[harga]
cost	harga	[harga]
sum	jumlah	[dʒ'umlah]

to spend (vt)	menghabiskan	[məɲhabiskan]
expenses	ongkos	[oŋkos]
to economize (vi, vt)	menghemat	[məɲhemat]
economical	hemat	[hemat]

to pay (vi, vt)	membayar	[membajar]
payment	pembayaran	[pembajaran]
change (give the ~)	kembalian	[kembalian]

tax	pajak	[padʒˈaˀ]
fine	denda	[denda]
to fine (vt)	mendenda	[məndenda]

81. Post. Postal service

post office	kantor pos	[kantor pos]
post (letters, etc.)	surat	[surat]
postman	tukang pos	[tukaŋ pos]
opening hours	jam buka	[dʒˈam buka]

letter	surat	[surat]
registered letter	surat tercatat	[surat tərtʃatat]
postcard	kartu pos	[kartu pos]
telegram	telegram	[telegram]
parcel	parsel, paket pos	[parsel], [paket pos]
money transfer	wesel pos	[wesel pos]

to receive (vt)	menerima	[mənerima]
to send (vt)	mengirim	[məɲirim]
sending	pengiriman	[peɲiriman]

address	alamat	[alamat]
postcode	kode pos	[kode pos]
sender	pengirim	[peɲirim]
receiver	penerima	[penerima]

| name (first name) | nama | [nama] |
| surname (last name) | nama keluarga | [nama keluarga] |

postage rate	tarif	[tarif]
standard (adj)	biasa, standar	[biasa], [standar]
economical (adj)	ekonomis	[ekonomis]

weight	berat	[berat]
to weigh (~ letters)	menimbang	[mənimbaŋ]
envelope	amplop	[amplop]
postage stamp	prangko	[praŋko]
to stamp an envelope	menempelkan prangko	[mənempelkan praŋko]

Dwelling. House. Home

82. House. Dwelling

house	rumah	[rumah]
at home (adv)	di rumah	[di rumah]
yard	pekarangan	[pekaraŋan]
fence (iron ~)	pagar	[pagar]
brick (n)	bata, batu bata	[bata], [batu bata]
brick (as adj)	bata, batu bata	[bata], [batu bata]
stone (n)	batu	[batu]
stone (as adj)	batu	[batu]
concrete (n)	beton	[beton]
concrete (as adj)	beton	[beton]
new (new-built)	baru	[baru]
old (adj)	tua	[tua]
decrepit (house)	reyot	[reyot]
modern (adj)	modern	[modern]
multistorey (adj)	susun	[susun]
tall (~ building)	tinggi	[tiŋgi]
floor, storey	lantai	[lantaj]
single-storey (adj)	berlantai satu	[bərlantaj satu]
ground floor	lantai bawah	[lantaj bawah]
top floor	lantai atas	[lantaj atas]
roof	atap	[atap]
chimney	cerobong	[ʧeroboŋ]
roof tiles	genting	[gentiŋ]
tiled (adj)	bergenting	[bərgentiŋ]
loft (attic)	loteng	[loteŋ]
window	jendela	[dʒʲendela]
glass	kaca	[kaʧa]
window ledge	ambang jendela	[ambaŋ dʒʲendela]
shutters	daun jendela	[daun dʒʲendela]
wall	dinding	[dindiŋ]
balcony	balkon	[balkon]
downpipe	pipa talang	[pipa talaŋ]
upstairs (to be ~)	di atas	[di atas]
to go upstairs	naik	[naiʔ]
to come down (the stairs)	turun	[turun]
to move (to new premises)	pindah	[pindah]

83. House. Entrance. Lift

entrance	**pintu masuk**	[pintu masu']
stairs (stairway)	**tangga**	[taŋga]
steps	**anak tangga**	[ana' taŋga]
banisters	**pegangan tangan**	[pegaŋan taŋan]
lobby (hotel ~)	**lobi, ruang depan**	[lobi], [ruaŋ depan]
postbox	**kotak pos**	[kota' pos]
waste bin	**tong sampah**	[toŋ sampah]
refuse chute	**saluran pembuangan sampah**	[saluran pembuaŋan sampah]
lift	**elevator**	[elevator]
goods lift	**lift barang**	[lift baraŋ]
lift cage	**kabin lift**	[kabin lift]
to take the lift	**naik elevator**	[nai' elevator]
flat	**apartemen**	[apartemen]
residents (~ of a building)	**penghuni**	[peŋhuni]
neighbour (masc.)	**tetangga**	[tetaŋga]
neighbour (fem.)	**tetangga**	[tetaŋga]
neighbours	**para tetangga**	[para tetaŋga]

84. House. Doors. Locks

door	**pintu**	[pintu]
gate (vehicle ~)	**pintu gerbang**	[pintu gerbaŋ]
handle, doorknob	**gagang pintu**	[gagaŋ pintu]
to unlock (unbolt)	**membuka kunci**	[membuka kuntʃi]
to open (vt)	**membuka**	[membuka]
to close (vt)	**menutup**	[menutup]
key	**kunci**	[kuntʃi]
bunch (of keys)	**serangkaian kunci**	[seraŋkajan kuntʃi]
to creak (door, etc.)	**bergerit**	[bergerit]
creak	**gerit**	[gerit]
hinge (door ~)	**engsel**	[eŋsel]
doormat	**tikar**	[tikar]
door lock	**kunci pintu**	[kuntʃi pintu]
keyhole	**lubang kunci**	[lubaŋ kuntʃi]
crossbar (sliding bar)	**gerendel**	[gerendel]
door latch	**gerendel**	[gerendel]
padlock	**gembok**	[gembo']
to ring (~ the door bell)	**membunyikan**	[membunjikan]
ringing (sound)	**dering**	[deriŋ]
doorbell	**bel**	[bel]
doorbell button	**kenop**	[kenop]
knock (at the door)	**ketukan**	[ketukan]
to knock (vi)	**mengetuk**	[meɲetu']

code	kode	[kode]
combination lock	gembok berkode	[gembo' bərkode]
intercom	interkom	[interkom]
number (on the door)	nomor	[nomor]
doorplate	papan tanda	[papan tanda]
peephole	lubang intip	[lubaŋ intip]

85. Country house

village	desa	[desa]
vegetable garden	kebun sayur	[kebun sajur]
fence	pagar	[pagar]
picket fence	pagar	[pagar]
wicket gate	pintu pagar	[pintu pagar]

granary	lumbung	[lumbuŋ]
cellar	kelder	[kelder]
shed (garden ~)	gubuk	[gubu']
water well	sumur	[sumur]

stove (wood-fired ~)	tungku	[tuŋku]
to stoke the stove	menyalakan tungku	[mənjalakan tuŋku]
firewood	kayu bakar	[kaju bakar]
log (firewood)	potongan kayu bakar	[potoŋan kaju bakar]

veranda	beranda	[bəranda]
deck (terrace)	teras	[teras]
stoop (front steps)	anjungan depan	[andʒ¡uŋan depan]
swing (hanging seat)	ayunan	[ajunan]

86. Castle. Palace

castle	kastil	[kastil]
palace	istana	[istana]
fortress	benteng	[benteŋ]

wall (round castle)	tembok	[tembo']
tower	menara	[mənara]
keep, donjon	menara utama	[mənara utama]

portcullis	jeruji pintu kota	[dʒ¡erudʒi pintu kota]
subterranean passage	jalan bawah tanah	[dʒ¡alan bawah tanah]
moat	parit	[parit]

| chain | rantai | [rantaj] |
| arrow loop | laras panah, lop panah | [laras panah], [lop panah] |

| magnificent (adj) | megah | [megah] |
| majestic (adj) | megah sekali | [megah sekali] |

| impregnable (adj) | sulit dicapai | [sulit ditʃapaj] |
| medieval (adj) | abad pertengahan | [abad pərteŋahan] |

87. Flat

flat	apartemen	[apartemen]
room	kamar	[kamar]
bedroom	kamar tidur	[kamar tidur]
dining room	ruang makan	[ruaŋ makan]
living room	ruang tamu	[ruaŋ tamu]
study (home office)	ruang kerja	[ruaŋ kerdʒˈa]
entry room	ruang depan	[ruaŋ depan]
bathroom	kamar mandi	[kamar mandi]
water closet	kamar kecil	[kamar ketʃil]
ceiling	plafon, langit-langit	[plafon], [laŋit-laŋit]
floor	lantai	[lantaj]
corner	sudut	[sudut]

88. Flat. Cleaning

to clean (vi, vt)	membereskan	[membereskan]
to put away (to stow)	meletakkan	[meletaʔkan]
dust	debu	[debu]
dusty (adj)	debu	[debu]
to dust (vt)	menyapu debu	[mənjapu debu]
vacuum cleaner	pengisap debu	[peŋisap debu]
to vacuum (vt)	membersihkan dengan pengisap debu	[membersihkan deŋan peŋisap debu]
to sweep (vi, vt)	menyapu	[mənjapu]
sweepings	sampah	[sampah]
order	kerapian	[kerapian]
disorder, mess	berantakan	[berantakan]
mop	kain pel	[kain pel]
duster	lap	[lap]
short broom	sapu lidi	[sapu lidi]
dustpan	pengki	[peŋki]

89. Furniture. Interior

furniture	mebel	[mebel]
table	meja	[medʒˈa]
chair	kursi	[kursi]
bed	ranjang	[randʒˈaŋ]
sofa, settee	dipan	[dipan]
armchair	kursi malas	[kursi malas]
bookcase	lemari buku	[lemari buku]
shelf	rak	[raʔ]
wardrobe	lemari pakaian	[lemari pakajan]

| coat rack (wall-mounted ~) | kapstok | [kapsto'] |
| coat stand | kapstok berdiri | [kapsto' berdiri] |

| chest of drawers | lemari laci | [lemari latʃi] |
| coffee table | meja kopi | [medʒ'a kopi] |

mirror	cermin	[tʃermin]
carpet	permadani	[pərmadani]
small carpet	karpet kecil	[karpet ketʃil]

fireplace	perapian	[pərapian]
candle	lilin	[lilin]
candlestick	kaki lilin	[kaki lilin]

drapes	gorden	[gorden]
wallpaper	kertas dinding	[kertas dindiŋ]
blinds (jalousie)	kerai	[keraj]

table lamp	lampu meja	[lampu medʒ'a]
wall lamp (sconce)	lampu dinding	[lampu dindiŋ]
standard lamp	lampu lantai	[lampu lantaj]
chandelier	lampu bercabang	[lampu bərtʃabaŋ]

leg (of a chair, table)	kaki	[kaki]
armrest	lengan	[leŋan]
back (backrest)	sandaran	[sandaran]
drawer	laci	[latʃi]

90. Bedding

bedclothes	kain kasur	[kain kasur]
pillow	bantal	[bantal]
pillowslip	sarung bantal	[saruŋ bantal]
duvet	selimut	[selimut]
sheet	seprai	[sepraj]
bedspread	selubung kasur	[selubuŋ kasur]

91. Kitchen

kitchen	dapur	[dapur]
gas	gas	[gas]
gas cooker	kompor gas	[kompor gas]
electric cooker	kompor listrik	[kompor listri']
oven	oven	[oven]
microwave oven	microwave	[majkrowav]

refrigerator	lemari es, kulkas	[lemari es], [kulkas]
freezer	lemari pembeku	[lemari pembeku]
dishwasher	mesin pencuci piring	[mesin pentʃutʃi piriŋ]

| mincer | alat pelumat daging | [alat pelumat dagiŋ] |
| juicer | mesin sari buah | [mesin sari buah] |

| toaster | alat pemanggang roti | [alat pemaŋgaŋ roti] |
| mixer | pencampur | [pentʃampur] |

coffee machine	mesin pembuat kopi	[mesin pembuat kopi]
coffee pot	teko kopi	[teko kopi]
coffee grinder	mesin penggiling kopi	[mesin peŋgiliŋ kopi]

kettle	cerek	[tʃereʔ]
teapot	teko	[teko]
lid	tutup	[tutup]
tea strainer	saringan teh	[sariŋan teh]

spoon	sendok	[sendoʔ]
teaspoon	sendok teh	[sendoʔ teh]
soup spoon	sendok makan	[sendoʔ makan]
fork	garpu	[garpu]
knife	pisau	[pisau]

tableware (dishes)	piring mangkuk	[piriŋ maŋkuʔ]
plate (dinner ~)	piring	[piriŋ]
saucer	alas cangkir	[alas tʃaŋkir]

shot glass	seloki	[seloki]
glass (tumbler)	gelas	[gelas]
cup	cangkir	[tʃaŋkir]

sugar bowl	wadah gula	[wadah gula]
salt cellar	wadah garam	[wadah garam]
pepper pot	wadah merica	[wadah meritʃa]
butter dish	wadah mentega	[wadah mentega]

stock pot (soup pot)	panci	[pantʃi]
frying pan (skillet)	kuali	[kuali]
ladle	sudu	[sudu]
colander	saringan	[sariŋan]
tray (serving ~)	talam	[talam]

bottle	botol	[botol]
jar (glass)	gelas	[gelas]
tin (can)	kaleng	[kaleŋ]

bottle opener	pembuka botol	[pembuka botol]
tin opener	pembuka kaleng	[pembuka kaleŋ]
corkscrew	kotrek	[kotreʔ]
filter	saringan	[sariŋan]
to filter (vt)	saringan	[sariŋan]

| waste (food ~, etc.) | sampah | [sampah] |
| waste bin (kitchen ~) | tong sampah | [toŋ sampah] |

92. Bathroom

| bathroom | kamar mandi | [kamar mandi] |
| water | air | [air] |

tap	keran	[keran]
hot water	air panas	[air panas]
cold water	air dingin	[air diŋin]
toothpaste	pasta gigi	[pasta gigi]
to clean one's teeth	menggosok gigi	[məŋgosoʔ gigi]
toothbrush	sikat gigi	[sikat gigi]
to shave (vi)	bercukur	[bərtʃukur]
shaving foam	busa cukur	[busa tʃukur]
razor	pisau cukur	[pisau tʃukur]
to wash (one's hands, etc.)	mencuci	[məntʃutʃi]
to have a bath	mandi	[mandi]
shower	pancuran	[pantʃuran]
to have a shower	mandi pancuran	[mandi pantʃuran]
bath	bak mandi	[baʔ mandi]
toilet (toilet bowl)	kloset	[kloset]
sink (washbasin)	wastafel	[wastafel]
soap	sabun	[sabun]
soap dish	wadah sabun	[wadah sabun]
sponge	spons	[spons]
shampoo	sampo	[sampo]
towel	handuk	[handuʔ]
bathrobe	jubah mandi	[dʒˈubah mandi]
laundry (laundering)	pencucian	[pentʃutʃian]
washing machine	mesin cuci	[mesin tʃutʃi]
to do the laundry	mencuci	[məntʃutʃi]
washing powder	deterjen cuci	[deterdʒˈen tʃutʃi]

93. Household appliances

TV, telly	pesawat TV	[pesawat ti-vi]
tape recorder	alat perekam	[alat pərekam]
video	video, VCR	[vidio], [vi-si-er]
radio	radio	[radio]
player (CD, MP3, etc.)	pemutar	[pemutar]
video projector	proyektor video	[proektor video]
home cinema	bioskop rumah	[bioskop rumah]
DVD player	pemutar DVD	[pemutar di-vi-di]
amplifier	penguat	[peŋuat]
video game console	konsol permainan video	[konsol pərmajnan video]
video camera	kamera video	[kamera video]
camera (photo)	kamera	[kamera]
digital camera	kamera digital	[kamera digital]
vacuum cleaner	pengisap debu	[peŋisap debu]
iron (e.g. steam ~)	setrika	[setrika]

ironing board	papan setrika	[papan setrika]
telephone	telepon	[telepon]
mobile phone	ponsel	[ponsel]
typewriter	mesin ketik	[mesin keti']
sewing machine	mesin jahit	[mesin dʒ¡ahit]

microphone	mikrofon	[mikrofon]
headphones	headphone, fonkepala	[headphone], [fonkepala]
remote control (TV)	panel kendali	[panel kendali]

CD, compact disc	cakram kompak	[tʃakram kompa']
cassette, tape	kaset	[kaset]
vinyl record	piringan hitam	[piriŋan hitam]

94. Repairs. Renovation

renovations	renovasi	[renovasi]
to renovate (vt)	merenovasi	[merenovasi]
to repair, to fix (vt)	mereparasi, memperbaiki	[mereparasi], [memperbajki]
to put in order	membereskan	[membereskan]
to redo (do again)	mengulangi	[məŋulaŋi]

paint	cat	[tʃat]
to paint (~ a wall)	mengecat	[məŋetʃat]
house painter	tukang cat	[tukaŋ tʃat]
paintbrush	kuas	[kuas]

| whitewash | cat kapur | [tʃat kapur] |
| to whitewash (vt) | mengapur | [məŋapur] |

wallpaper	kertas dinding	[kertas dindiŋ]
to wallpaper (vt)	memasang kertas dinding	[memasaŋ kertas dindiŋ]
varnish	pernis	[pernis]
to varnish (vt)	memernis	[memernis]

95. Plumbing

water	air	[air]
hot water	air panas	[air panas]
cold water	air dingin	[air diŋin]
tap	keran	[keran]

drop (of water)	tetes	[tetes]
to drip (vi)	menetes	[mənetes]
to leak (ab. pipe)	bocor	[botʃor]
leak (pipe ~)	kebocoran	[kebotʃoran]
puddle	kubangan	[kubaŋan]

pipe	pipa	[pipa]
valve (e.g., ball ~)	katup	[katup]
to be clogged up	tersumbat	[tərsumbat]
tools	peralatan	[pəralatan]

adjustable spanner	kunci inggris	[kuntʃi iŋgris]
to unscrew (lid, filter, etc.)	mengendurkan	[məŋendurkan]
to screw (tighten)	mengencangkan	[məŋentʃaŋkan]

to unclog (vt)	membersihkan	[membersihkan]
plumber	tukang pipa	[tukaŋ pipa]
basement	rubanah	[rubanah]
sewerage (system)	riol	[riol]

96. Fire. Conflagration

fire (accident)	kebakaran	[kebakaran]
flame	nyala api	[njala api]
spark	percikan api	[pərtʃikan api]
smoke (from fire)	asap	[asap]
torch (flaming stick)	obor	[obor]
campfire	api unggun	[api uŋgun]

petrol	bensin	[bensin]
paraffin	minyak tanah	[minja' tanah]
flammable (adj)	mudah terbakar	[mudah tərbakar]
explosive (adj)	mudah meledak	[mudah meleda']
NO SMOKING	DILARANG MEROKOK!	[dilaraŋ meroko'!]

safety	keamanan	[keamanan]
danger	bahaya	[bahaja]
dangerous (adj)	berbahaya	[bərbahaja]

to catch fire	menyala	[mənjala]
explosion	ledakan	[ledakan]
to set fire	membakar	[membakar]
arsonist	pelaku pembakaran	[pelaku pembakaran]
arson	pembakaran	[pembakaran]

to blaze (vi)	berkobar	[bərkobar]
to burn (be on fire)	menyala	[mənjala]
to burn down	terbakar	[tərbakar]

| to call the fire brigade | memanggil pemadam kebakaran | [memaŋgil pemadam kebakaran] |

firefighter, fireman	pemadam kebakaran	[pemadam kebakaran]
fire engine	branwir	[branwir]
fire brigade	pemadam kebakaran	[pemadam kebakaran]
fire engine ladder	tangga branwir	[taŋga branwir]

fire hose	selang pemadam	[selaŋ pemadam]
fire extinguisher	pemadam api	[pemadam api]
helmet	helm	[helm]
siren	sirene	[sirene]

to cry (for help)	berteriak	[bərteria']
to call for help	meminta pertolongan	[meminta pərtoloŋan]
rescuer	penyelamat	[penjelamat]
to rescue (vt)	menyelamatkan	[mənjelamatkan]

to arrive (vi)	**datang**	[dataŋ]
to extinguish (vt)	**memadamkan**	[memadamkan]
water	**air**	[air]
sand	**pasir**	[pasir]

ruins (destruction)	**reruntuhan**	[reruntuhan]
to collapse (building, etc.)	**runtuh**	[runtuh]
to fall down (vi)	**roboh**	[roboh]
to cave in (ceiling, floor)	**roboh**	[roboh]

piece of debris	**serpihan**	[serpihan]
ash	**abu**	[abu]

to suffocate (die)	**mati lemas**	[mati lemas]
to be killed (perish)	**mati, tewas**	[mati], [tewas]

HUMAN ACTIVITIES

Job. Business. Part 1

97. Banking

bank	**bank**	[banˀ]
branch (of a bank)	**cabang**	[tʃabaŋ]
consultant	**konsultan**	[konsultan]
manager (director)	**manajer**	[manadʒʲer]
bank account	**rekening**	[rekeniŋ]
account number	**nomor rekening**	[nomor rekeniŋ]
current account	**rekening koran**	[rekeniŋ koran]
deposit account	**rekening simpanan**	[rekeniŋ simpanan]
to open an account	**membuka rekening**	[membuka rekeniŋ]
to close the account	**menutup rekening**	[mənutup rekeniŋ]
to deposit into the account	**memasukkan ke rekening**	[memasuˀkan ke rekeniŋ]
to withdraw (vt)	**menarik uang**	[mənariˀ uaŋ]
deposit	**deposito**	[deposito]
to make a deposit	**melakukan setoran**	[melakukan setoran]
wire transfer	**transfer kawat**	[transfer kawat]
to wire, to transfer	**mentransfer**	[məntransfer]
sum	**jumlah**	[dʒʲumlah]
How much?	**Berapa?**	[bərapa?]
signature	**tanda tangan**	[tanda taŋan]
to sign (vt)	**menandatangani**	[mənandataŋani]
credit card	**kartu kredit**	[kartu kredit]
code (PIN code)	**kode**	[kode]
credit card number	**nomor kartu kredit**	[nomor kartu kredit]
cashpoint	**Anjungan Tunai Mandiri, ATM**	[andʒʲuŋan tunaj mandiri], [a-te-em]
cheque	**cek**	[tʃeˀ]
to write a cheque	**menulis cek**	[mənulis tʃeˀ]
chequebook	**buku cek**	[buku tʃeˀ]
loan (bank ~)	**kredit, pinjaman**	[kredit], [pindʒʲaman]
to apply for a loan	**meminta kredit**	[meminta kredit]
to get a loan	**mendapatkan kredit**	[məndapatkan kredit]
to give a loan	**memberikan kredit**	[memberikan kredit]
guarantee	**jaminan**	[dʒʲaminan]

98. Telephone. Phone conversation

telephone	telepon	[telepon]
mobile phone	ponsel	[ponsel]
answerphone	mesin penjawab panggilan	[mesin pendʒawab paŋgilan]
to call (by phone)	menelepon	[mənelepon]
call, ring	panggilan telepon	[paŋgilan telepon]
to dial a number	memutar nomor telepon	[memutar nomor telepon]
Hello!	Halo!	[halo!]
to ask (vt)	bertanya	[bərtanja]
to answer (vi, vt)	menjawab	[məndʒawab]
to hear (vt)	mendengar	[məndeŋar]
well (adv)	baik	[baj']
not well (adv)	buruk, jelek	[buruk], [dʒele']
noises (interference)	bising, gangguan	[bisiŋ], [gaŋguan]
receiver	gagang	[gagaŋ]
to pick up (~ the phone)	mengangkat telepon	[məŋaŋkat telepon]
to hang up (~ the phone)	menutup telepon	[mənutup telepon]
busy (engaged)	sibuk	[sibu']
to ring (ab. phone)	berdering	[bərderiŋ]
telephone book	buku telepon	[buku telepon]
local (adj)	lokal	[lokal]
local call	panggilan lokal	[paŋgilan lokal]
trunk (e.g. ~ call)	interlokal	[interlokal]
trunk call	panggilan interlokal	[paŋgilan interlokal]
international (adj)	internasional	[internasional]
international call	panggilan internasional	[paŋgilan internasional]

99. Mobile telephone

mobile phone	ponsel	[ponsel]
display	layar	[lajar]
button	kenop	[kenop]
SIM card	kartu SIM	[kartu sim]
battery	baterai	[bateraj]
to be flat (battery)	mati	[mati]
charger	pengisi baterai, pengecas	[peŋisi bateraj], [peɲetʃas]
menu	menu	[menu]
settings	penyetelan	[penjetelan]
tune (melody)	nada panggil	[nada paŋgil]
to select (vt)	memilih	[memilih]
calculator	kalkulator	[kalkulator]
voice mail	penjawab telepon	[pendʒawab telepon]
alarm clock	weker	[weker]

contacts	buku telepon	[buku telepon]
SMS (text message)	pesan singkat	[pesan siŋkat]
subscriber	pelanggan	[pelaŋgan]

100. Stationery

| ballpoint pen | bolpen | [bolpen] |
| fountain pen | pena celup | [pena tʃelup] |

pencil	pensil	[pensil]
highlighter	spidol	[spidol]
felt-tip pen	spidol	[spidol]

| notepad | buku catatan | [buku tʃatatan] |
| diary | agenda | [agenda] |

ruler	mistar, penggaris	[mistar], [peŋgaris]
calculator	kalkulator	[kalkulator]
rubber	karet penghapus	[karet peŋhapus]
drawing pin	paku payung	[paku pajuŋ]
paper clip	penjepit kertas	[pendʒepit kertas]

glue	lem	[lem]
stapler	stapler	[stapler]
hole punch	alat pelubang kertas	[alat pelubaŋ kertas]
pencil sharpener	rautan pensil	[rautan pensil]

Job. Business. Part 2

101. Mass Media

newspaper	koran	[koran]
magazine	majalah	[madʒi̯alah]
press (printed media)	pers	[pers]
radio	radio	[radio]
radio station	stasiun radio	[stasiun radio]
television	televisi	[televisi]
presenter, host	pembawa acara	[pembawa atʃara]
newsreader	penyiar	[penjiar]
commentator	komentator	[komentator]
journalist	wartawan	[wartawan]
correspondent (reporter)	koresponden	[koresponden]
press photographer	fotografer pers	[fotografer pərs]
reporter	reporter, pewarta	[reporter], [pewarta]
editor	editor, penyunting	[editor], [penyuntiŋ]
editor-in-chief	editor kepala	[editor kepala]
to subscribe (to …)	berlangganan …	[bərlaŋganan …]
subscription	langganan	[laŋganan]
subscriber	pelanggan	[pelaŋgan]
to read (vi, vt)	membaca	[membatʃa]
reader	pembaca	[pembatʃa]
circulation (of a newspaper)	oplah	[oplah]
monthly (adj)	bulanan	[bulanan]
weekly (adj)	mingguan	[miŋguan]
issue (edition)	edisi	[edisi]
new (~ issue)	baru	[baru]
headline	kepala berita	[kepala bərita]
short article	artikel singkat	[artikel siŋkat]
column (regular article)	kolom	[kolom]
article	artikel	[artikel]
page	halaman	[halaman]
reportage, report	reportase	[reportase]
event (happening)	peristiwa, kejadian	[peristiwa], [kedʒi̯adian]
sensation (news)	sensasi	[sensasi]
scandal	skandal	[skandal]
scandalous (adj)	penuh skandal	[penuh skandal]
great (~ scandal)	besar	[besar]
programme (e.g. cooking ~)	program	[program]
interview	wawancara	[wawantʃara]

| live broadcast | siaran langsung | [siaran laŋsuŋ] |
| channel | saluran | [saluran] |

102. Agriculture

agriculture	pertanian	[pərtanian]
peasant (masc.)	petani	[petani]
peasant (fem.)	petani	[petani]
farmer	petani	[petani]

| tractor | traktor | [traktor] |
| combine, harvester | mesin pemanen | [mesin pemanen] |

plough	bajak	[badʒˡaʔ]
to plough (vi, vt)	membajak, menenggala	[membadʒˡak], [menəŋgala]
ploughland	tanah garapan	[tanah garapan]
furrow (in field)	alur	[alur]

to sow (vi, vt)	menanam	[mənanam]
seeder	mesin penanam	[mesin penanam]
sowing (process)	penanaman	[penanaman]

| scythe | sabit | [sabit] |
| to mow, to scythe | menyabit | [mənjabit] |

| spade (tool) | sekop | [sekop] |
| to till (vt) | menggali | [məŋgali] |

hoe	cangkul	[tʃaŋkul]
to hoe, to weed	menyiangi	[mənjiaŋi]
weed (plant)	gulma	[gulma]

watering can	kaleng penyiram	[kaleŋ penjiram]
to water (plants)	menyiram	[mənjiram]
watering (act)	penyiraman	[penjiraman]

| pitchfork | garpu ramput | [garpu ramput] |
| rake | penggaruk | [peŋgaruʔ] |

fertiliser	pupuk	[pupuʔ]
to fertilise (vt)	memupuk	[memupuʔ]
manure (fertiliser)	pupuk kandang	[pupuʔ kandaŋ]

field	ladang	[ladaŋ]
meadow	padang rumput	[padaŋ rumput]
vegetable garden	kebun sayur	[kebun sajur]
orchard (e.g. apple ~)	kebun buah	[kebun buah]

to graze (vt)	menggembalakan	[məŋgembalakan]
herdsman	penggembala	[peŋgembala]
pasture	padang penggembalaan	[padaŋ peŋgembalaʔan]

| cattle breeding | peternakan | [peternakan] |
| sheep farming | peternakan domba | [peternakan domba] |

plantation	perkebunan	[pərkebunan]
row (garden bed ~s)	bedeng	[bedeŋ]
hothouse	rumah kaca	[rumah katʃa]

| drought (lack of rain) | musim kering | [musim keriŋ] |
| dry (~ summer) | kering | [keriŋ] |

grain	biji	[bidʒi]
cereal crops	serealia	[serealia]
to harvest, to gather	memanen	[memanen]

miller (person)	penggiling	[peŋgiliŋ]
mill (e.g. gristmill)	kincir	[kintʃir]
to grind (grain)	menggiling	[meŋgiliŋ]
flour	tepung	[tepuŋ]
straw	jerami	[dʒerami]

103. Building. Building process

building site	lokasi pembangunan	[lokasi pembaŋunan]
to build (vt)	membangun	[membaŋun]
building worker	buruh bangunan	[buruh baŋunan]

project	proyek	[proeʔ]
architect	arsitek	[arsiteʔ]
worker	buruh, pekerja	[buruh], [pekerdʒa]

foundations (of a building)	fondasi	[fondasi]
roof	atap	[atap]
foundation pile	tiang fondasi	[tiaŋ fondasi]
wall	dinding	[dindiŋ]

| reinforcing bars | kerangka besi | [keraŋka besi] |
| scaffolding | perancah | [perantʃah] |

concrete	beton	[beton]
granite	granit	[granit]
stone	batu	[batu]
brick	bata, batu bata	[bata], [batu bata]

sand	pasir	[pasir]
cement	semen	[semen]
plaster (for walls)	lepa, plester	[lepa], [plester]
to plaster (vt)	melepa	[melepa]
paint	cat	[tʃat]
to paint (~ a wall)	mengecat	[meŋetʃat]
barrel	tong	[toŋ]

crane	derek	[dereʔ]
to lift, to hoist (vt)	menaikkan	[menajʔkan]
to lower (vt)	menurunkan	[menurunkan]

| bulldozer | buldoser | [buldozer] |
| excavator | ekskavator | [ekskavator] |

scoop, bucket	**sudu pengeruk**	[sudu peŋeruʔ]
to dig (excavate)	**menggali**	[məŋgali]
hard hat	**topi baja**	[topi badʒʲa]

Professions and occupations

job	kerja, pekerjaan	[kerdʒʲa], [pekerdʒʲaʼan]
staff (work force)	staf, personalia	[staf], [pərsonalia]
personnel	staf, personel	[staf], [pərsonel]

career	karier	[karier]
prospects (chances)	perspektif	[pərspektif]
skills (mastery)	keterampilan	[keterampilan]

selection (screening)	pilihan	[pilihan]
employment agency	biro tenaga kerja	[biro tenaga kerdʒʲa]
curriculum vitae, CV	resume	[resume]
job interview	wawancara kerja	[wawantʃara kerdʒʲa]
vacancy	lowongan	[lowoŋan]

salary, pay	gaji, upah	[gadʒi], [upah]
fixed salary	gaji tetap	[gadʒi tetap]
pay, compensation	bayaran	[bajaran]

position (job)	jabatan	[dʒʲabatan]
duty (of an employee)	tugas	[tugas]
range of duties	bidang tugas	[bidaŋ tugas]
busy (I'm ~)	sibuk	[sibuʔ]

| to fire (dismiss) | memecat | [memetʃat] |
| dismissal | pemecatan | [pemetʃatan] |

unemployment	pengangguran	[peŋaŋguran]
unemployed (n)	pengganggur	[peŋaŋgur]
retirement	pensiun	[pensiun]
to retire (from job)	pensiun	[pensiun]

director	direktur	[direktur]
manager (director)	manajer	[manadʒʲer]
boss	bos, atasan	[bos], [atasan]

superior	atasan	[atasan]
superiors	atasan	[atasan]
president	presiden	[presiden]
chairman	ketua, dirut	[ketua], [dirut]

| deputy (substitute) | wakil | [wakil] |
| assistant | asisten | [asisten] |

secretary	sekretaris	[sekretaris]
personal assistant	asisten pribadi	[asisten pribadi]
businessman	pengusaha, pebisnis	[peŋusaha], [pebisnis]
entrepreneur	pengusaha	[peŋusaha]
founder	pendiri	[pendiri]
to found (vt)	mendirikan	[məndirikan]
founding member	pendiri	[pendiri]
partner	mitra	[mitra]
shareholder	pemegang saham	[pemegaŋ saham]
millionaire	jutawan	[dʒutawan]
billionaire	miliarder	[miliarder]
owner, proprietor	pemilik	[pemiliʔ]
landowner	tuan tanah	[tuan tanah]
client	klien	[klien]
regular client	klien tetap	[klien tetap]
buyer (customer)	pembeli	[pembeli]
visitor	tamu	[tamu]
professional (n)	profesional	[profesional]
expert	pakar, ahli	[pakar], [ahli]
specialist	spesialis, ahli	[spesialis], [ahli]
banker	bankir	[bankir]
broker	broker, pialang	[broker], [pialaŋ]
cashier	kasir	[kasir]
accountant	akuntan	[akuntan]
security guard	satpam, pengawal	[satpam], [peŋawal]
investor	investor	[investor]
debtor	debitur	[debitur]
creditor	kreditor	[kreditor]
borrower	peminjam	[pemindʒam]
importer	importir	[importir]
exporter	eksportir	[eksportir]
manufacturer	produsen	[produsen]
distributor	penyalur	[penjalur]
middleman	perantara	[pərantara]
consultant	konsultan	[konsultan]
sales representative	perwakilan penjualan	[pərwakilan pendʒualan]
agent	agen	[agen]
insurance agent	agen asuransi	[agen asuransi]

106. Service professions

| cook | koki, juru masak | [koki], [dʒuru masaʔ] |
| chef (kitchen chef) | koki kepala | [koki kepala] |

baker	pembuat roti	[pembuat roti]
barman	pelayan bar	[pelajan bar]
waiter	pelayan lelaki	[pelajan lelaki]
waitress	pelayan perempuan	[pelajan perempuan]

lawyer, barrister	advokat, pengacara	[advokat], [peŋatʃara]
lawyer (legal expert)	ahli hukum	[ahli hukum]
notary public	notaris	[notaris]

electrician	tukang listrik	[tukaŋ listriʔ]
plumber	tukang pipa	[tukaŋ pipa]
carpenter	tukang kayu	[tukaŋ kaju]

masseur	tukang pijat lelaki	[tukaŋ pidʒⁱat lelaki]
masseuse	tukang pijat perempuan	[tukaŋ pidʒⁱat perempuan]
doctor	dokter	[dokter]

taxi driver	sopir taksi	[sopir taksi]
driver	sopir	[sopir]
delivery man	kurir	[kurir]

chambermaid	pelayan kamar	[pelajan kamar]
security guard	satpam, pengawal	[satpam], [peŋawal]
flight attendant (fem.)	pramugari	[pramugari]

schoolteacher	guru	[guru]
librarian	pustakawan	[pustakawan]
translator	penerjemah	[penerdʒⁱemah]
interpreter	juru bahasa	[dʒⁱuru bahasa]
guide	pemandu wisata	[pemandu wisata]

hairdresser	tukang cukur	[tukaŋ tʃukur]
postman	tukang pos	[tukaŋ pos]
salesman (store staff)	pramuniaga	[pramuniaga]

gardener	tukang kebun	[tukaŋ kebun]
domestic servant	pramuwisma	[pramuwisma]
maid (female servant)	pramuwisma	[pramuwisma]
cleaner (cleaning lady)	pembersih ruangan	[pembersih ruaŋan]

107. Military professions and ranks

private	prajurit	[pradʒⁱurit]
sergeant	sersan	[sersan]
lieutenant	letnan	[letnan]
captain	kapten	[kapten]

major	mayor	[major]
colonel	kolonel	[kolonel]
general	jenderal	[dʒⁱenderal]
marshal	marsekal	[marsekal]
admiral	laksamana	[laksamana]
military (n)	anggota militer	[aŋgota militer]
soldier	tentara, serdadu	[tentara], [serdadu]

| officer | perwira | [pərwira] |
| commander | komandan | [komandan] |

border guard	penjaga perbatasan	[pendʒʲaga pərbatasan]
radio operator	operator radio	[operator radio]
scout (searcher)	pengintai	[peɲintaj]
pioneer (sapper)	pencari ranjau	[pentʃari randʒʲau]
marksman	petembak	[petembaʔ]
navigator	navigator, penavigasi	[navigator], [penavigasi]

108. Officials. Priests

| king | raja | [radʒʲa] |
| queen | ratu | [ratu] |

| prince | pangeran | [paŋeran] |
| princess | putri | [putri] |

| czar | tsar, raja | [tsar], [radʒʲa] |
| czarina | tsarina, ratu | [tsarina], [ratu] |

president	presiden	[presiden]
Secretary (minister)	Menteri Sekretaris	[mənteri sekretaris]
prime minister	perdana menteri	[pərdana menteri]
senator	senator	[senator]

diplomat	diplomat	[diplomat]
consul	konsul	[konsul]
ambassador	duta besar	[duta besar]
counselor (diplomatic officer)	penasihat	[penasihat]

official, functionary (civil servant)	petugas	[petugas]
prefect	prefek	[prefeʔ]
mayor	walikota	[walikota]

| judge | hakim | [hakim] |
| prosecutor | kejaksaan negeri | [kedʒʲaksaʔan negeri] |

missionary	misionaris	[misionaris]
monk	biarawan, rahib	[biarawan], [rahib]
abbot	abbas	[abbas]
rabbi	rabbi	[rabbi]

vizier	wazir	[wazir]
shah	syah	[ʃah]
sheikh	syeikh	[ʃejh]

109. Agricultural professions

| beekeeper | peternak lebah | [peternaʔ lebah] |
| shepherd | penggembala | [peŋgembala] |

agronomist	**agronom**	[agronom]
cattle breeder	**peternak**	[peterna?]
veterinary surgeon	**dokter hewan**	[dokter hewan]

farmer	**petani**	[petani]
winemaker	**pembuat anggur**	[pembuat aŋgur]
zoologist	**zoolog**	[zoolog]
cowboy	**koboi**	[koboi]

110. Art professions

actor	**aktor**	[aktor]
actress	**aktris**	[aktris]

singer (masc.)	**biduan**	[biduan]
singer (fem.)	**biduanita**	[biduanita]

dancer (masc.)	**penari lelaki**	[penari lelaki]
dancer (fem.)	**penari perempuan**	[penari pərempuan]

performer (masc.)	**artis**	[artis]
performer (fem.)	**artis**	[artis]

musician	**musisi, musikus**	[musisi], [musikus]
pianist	**pianis**	[pianis]
guitar player	**pemain gitar**	[pemajn gitar]

conductor (orchestra ~)	**konduktor**	[konduktor]
composer	**komposer, komponis**	[komposer], [komponis]
impresario	**impresario**	[impresario]

film director	**sutradara**	[sutradara]
producer	**produser**	[produser]
scriptwriter	**penulis skenario**	[penulis skenario]
critic	**kritikus**	[kritikus]

writer	**penulis**	[penulis]
poet	**penyair**	[penjajr]
sculptor	**pematung**	[pematuŋ]
artist (painter)	**perupa**	[pərupa]

juggler	**juggler**	[dʒ'uggler]
clown	**badut**	[badut]
acrobat	**akrobat**	[akrobat]
magician	**pesulap**	[pesulap]

111. Various professions

doctor	**dokter**	[dokter]
nurse	**suster, juru rawat**	[suster], [dʒ'uru rawat]
psychiatrist	**psikiater**	[psikiater]
dentist	**dokter gigi**	[dokter gigi]

surgeon	dokter bedah	[dokter bedah]
astronaut	astronaut	[astronaut]
astronomer	astronom	[astronom]
pilot	pilot	[pilot]
driver (of a taxi, etc.)	sopir	[sopir]
train driver	masinis	[masinis]
mechanic	mekanik	[mekaniʔ]
miner	penambang	[penambaŋ]
worker	buruh, pekerja	[buruh], [pekerdʒia]
locksmith	tukang kikir	[tukaŋ kikir]
joiner (carpenter)	tukang kayu	[tukaŋ kaju]
turner (lathe operator)	tukang bubut	[tukaŋ bubut]
building worker	buruh bangunan	[buruh baŋunan]
welder	tukang las	[tukaŋ las]
professor (title)	profesor	[profesor]
architect	arsitek	[arsiteʔ]
historian	sejarawan	[sedʒiarawan]
scientist	ilmuwan	[ilmuwan]
physicist	fisikawan	[fisikawan]
chemist (scientist)	kimiawan	[kimiawan]
archaeologist	arkeolog	[arkeolog]
geologist	geolog	[geolog]
researcher (scientist)	periset, peneliti	[periset], [peneliti]
babysitter	pengasuh anak	[peŋasuh anaʔ]
teacher, educator	guru, pendidik	[guru], [pendidiʔ]
editor	editor, penyunting	[editor], [penyuntiŋ]
editor-in-chief	editor kepala	[editor kepala]
correspondent	koresponden	[koresponden]
typist (fem.)	juru ketik	[dʒiuru ketiʔ]
designer	desainer, perancang	[desajner], [perantʃaŋ]
computer expert	ahli komputer	[ahli komputer]
programmer	pemrogram	[pemrogram]
engineer (designer)	insinyur	[insinyur]
sailor	pelaut	[pelaut]
seaman	kelasi	[kelasi]
rescuer	penyelamat	[penjelamat]
firefighter	pemadam kebakaran	[pemadam kebakaran]
police officer	polisi	[polisi]
watchman	penjaga	[pendʒiaga]
detective	detektif	[detektif]
customs officer	petugas pabean	[petugas pabean]
bodyguard	pengawal pribadi	[peŋawal pribadi]
prison officer	sipir, penjaga penjara	[sipir], [pendʒiaga pendʒiara]
inspector	inspektur	[inspektur]
sportsman	olahragawan	[olahragawan]
trainer, coach	pelatih	[pelatih]

butcher	tukang daging	[tukaŋ dagiŋ]
cobbler (shoe repairer)	tukang sepatu	[tukaŋ sepatu]
merchant	pedagang	[pedagaŋ]
loader (person)	kuli	[kuli]

| fashion designer | perancang busana | [pərantʃaŋ busana] |
| model (fem.) | peragawati | [pəragawati] |

112. Occupations. Social status

| schoolboy | siswa | [siswa] |
| student (college ~) | mahasiswa | [mahasiswa] |

philosopher	filsuf	[filsuf]
economist	ahli ekonomi	[ahli ekonomi]
inventor	penemu	[penemu]

unemployed (n)	pengganggur	[peŋgaŋgur]
retiree, pensioner	pensiunan	[pensiunan]
spy, secret agent	mata-mata	[mata-mata]

prisoner	tahanan	[tahanan]
striker	pemogok	[pemogoʔ]
bureaucrat	birokrat	[birokrat]
traveller (globetrotter)	pelancong	[pelantʃoŋ]

gay, homosexual (n)	homo, homoseksual	[homo], [homoseksual]
hacker	peretas	[pəretas]
hippie	hipi	[hipi]

bandit	bandit	[bandit]
hit man, killer	pembunuh bayaran	[pembunuh bajaran]
drug addict	pecandu narkoba	[petʃandu narkoba]
drug dealer	pengedar narkoba	[peŋedar narkoba]
prostitute (fem.)	pelacur	[pelatʃur]
pimp	germo	[germo]

sorcerer	penyihir lelaki	[penjihir lelaki]
sorceress (evil ~)	penyihir perempuan	[penjihir pərempuan]
pirate	bajak laut	[badʒiaʔ laut]
slave	budak	[budaʔ]
samurai	samurai	[samuraj]
savage (primitive)	orang primitif	[oraŋ primitif]

Sports

sportsman	olahragawan	[olahragawan]
kind of sport	jenis olahraga	[dʒʲenis olahraga]
basketball	bola basket	[bola basket]
basketball player	pemain bola basket	[pemajn bola basket]
baseball	bisbol	[bisbol]
baseball player	pemain bisbol	[pemajn bisbol]
football	sepak bola	[sepaʔ bola]
football player	pemain sepak bola	[pemajn sepaʔ bola]
goalkeeper	kiper, penjaga gawang	[kiper], [pendʒʲaga gawaŋ]
ice hockey	hoki	[hoki]
ice hockey player	pemain hoki	[pemajn hoki]
volleyball	bola voli	[bola voli]
volleyball player	pemain bola voli	[pemajn bola voli]
boxing	tinju	[tindʒʲu]
boxer	petinju	[petindʒʲu]
wrestling	gulat	[gulat]
wrestler	pegulat	[pegulat]
karate	karate	[karate]
karate fighter	karateka	[karateka]
judo	judo	[dʒʲudo]
judo athlete	pejudo	[pedʒʲudo]
tennis	tenis	[tenis]
tennis player	petenis	[petenis]
swimming	berenang	[bərenaŋ]
swimmer	perenang	[pərenaŋ]
fencing	anggar	[aŋgar]
fencer	pemain anggar	[pemajn aŋgar]
chess	catur	[tʃatur]
chess player	pecatur	[petʃatur]
alpinism	mendaki gunung	[məndaki gunuŋ]
alpinist	pendaki gunung	[pendaki gunuŋ]
running	lari	[lari]

runner	**pelari**	[pelari]
athletics	**atletik**	[atletiʔ]
athlete	**atlet**	[atlet]
horse riding	**menunggang kuda**	[mənuŋgaŋ kuda]
horse rider	**penunggang kuda**	[penuŋgaŋ kuda]
figure skating	**seluncur indah**	[seluntʃur indah]
figure skater (masc.)	**peseluncur indah**	[peseluntʃur indah]
figure skater (fem.)	**peseluncur indah**	[peseluntʃur indah]
powerlifting	**angkat berat**	[aŋkat bərat]
powerlifter	**atlet angkat berat**	[atlet aŋkat bərat]
car racing	**balapan mobil**	[balapan mobil]
racer (driver)	**pembalap mobil**	[pembalap mobil]
cycling	**bersepeda**	[bərsepeda]
cyclist	**atlet sepeda**	[atlet sepeda]
long jump	**lompat jauh**	[lompat dʒʲauh]
pole vaulting	**lompat galah**	[lompat galah]
jumper	**atlet lompat, pelompat**	[atlet lompat], [pelompat]

114. Kinds of sports. Miscellaneous

American football	**futbol**	[futbol]
badminton	**badminton, bulu tangkis**	[badminton], [bulu taŋkis]
biathlon	**biathlon**	[biatlon]
billiards	**biliar**	[biliar]
bobsleigh	**bobsled**	[bobsled]
bodybuilding	**binaraga**	[binaraga]
water polo	**polo air**	[polo air]
handball	**bola tangan**	[bola taŋan]
golf	**golf**	[golf]
rowing	**mendayung**	[məndajuŋ]
scuba diving	**selam skuba**	[selam skuba]
cross-country skiing	**ski lintas alam**	[ski lintas alam]
table tennis (ping-pong)	**tenis meja**	[tenis medʒʲa]
sailing	**berlayar**	[bərlajar]
rally	**balap reli**	[balap reli]
rugby	**rugbi**	[rugbi]
snowboarding	**seluncur salju**	[seluntʃur saldʒʲu]
archery	**memanah**	[memanah]

115. Gym

barbell	**barbel**	[barbel]
dumbbells	**dumbel**	[dumbel]

training machine	alat senam	[alat senam]
exercise bicycle	sepeda statis	[sepeda statis]
treadmill	treadmill	[tredmil]

horizontal bar	rekstok	[reksto']
parallel bars	palang sejajar	[palaŋ sedʒʲadʒʲar]
vault (vaulting horse)	kuda-kuda	[kuda-kuda]
mat (exercise ~)	matras	[matras]

skipping rope	lompat tali	[lompat tali]
aerobics	aerobik	[aerobi']
yoga	yoga	[yoga]

116. Sports. Miscellaneous

Olympic Games	Olimpiade	[olimpiade]
winner	pemenang	[pemenaŋ]
to be winning	unggul	[uŋgul]
to win (vi)	menang	[menaŋ]

| leader | pemimpin | [pemimpin] |
| to lead (vi) | memimpin | [memimpin] |

first place	tempat pertama	[tempat pərtama]
second place	tempat kedua	[tempat kedua]
third place	tempat ketiga	[tempat ketiga]

medal	medali	[medali]
trophy	trofi	[trofi]
prize cup (trophy)	piala	[piala]
prize (in game)	hadiah	[hadiah]
main prize	hadiah utama	[hadiah utama]

| record | rekor | [rekor] |
| to set a record | menciptakan rekor | [məntʃiptakan rekor] |

| final | final | [final] |
| final (adj) | final | [final] |

| champion | juara | [dʒʲuara] |
| championship | kejuaraan | [kedʒʲuara'an] |

stadium	stadion	[stadion]
terrace	tribun	[tribun]
fan, supporter	pendukung	[pendukuŋ]
opponent, rival	lawan	[lawan]

| start (start line) | start | [start] |
| finish line | finis | [finis] |

defeat	kekalahan	[kekalahan]
to lose (not win)	kalah	[kalah]
referee	wasit	[wasit]
jury (judges)	juri	[dʒʲuri]

score	skor	[skor]
draw	seri, hasil imbang	[seri], [hasil imbaŋ]
to draw (vi)	bermain seri	[bərmajn seri]
point	poin	[poin]
result (final score)	skor, hasil akhir	[skor], [hasil ahir]

| period | babak | [baba'] |
| half-time | waktu istirahat | [waktu istirahat] |

doping	doping	[dopiŋ]
to penalise (vt)	menghukum	[məŋhukum]
to disqualify (vt)	mendiskualifikasi	[məndiskualifikasi]

apparatus	alat olahraga	[alat olahraga]
javelin	lembing	[lembiŋ]
shot (metal ball)	peluru	[peluru]
ball (snooker, etc.)	bola	[bola]

aim (target)	sasaran	[sasaran]
target	sasaran	[sasaran]
to shoot (vi)	menembak	[mənemba']
accurate (~ shot)	akurat	[akurat]

trainer, coach	pelatih	[pelatih]
to train (sb)	melatih	[melatih]
to train (vi)	berlatih	[bərlatih]
training	latihan	[latihan]

gym	gimnasium	[gimnasium]
exercise (physical)	latihan	[latihan]
warm-up (athlete ~)	pemanasan	[pemanasan]

Education

school	**sekolah**	[sekolah]
headmaster	**kepala sekolah**	[kepala sekolah]
student (m)	**murid laki-laki**	[murid laki-laki]
student (f)	**murid perempuan**	[murid perempuan]
schoolboy	**siswa**	[siswa]
schoolgirl	**siswi**	[siswi]
to teach (sb)	**mengajar**	[məŋadʒ'ar]
to learn (language, etc.)	**belajar**	[beladʒ'ar]
to learn by heart	**menghafalkan**	[məŋhafalkan]
to learn (~ to count, etc.)	**belajar**	[beladʒ'ar]
to be at school	**bersekolah**	[bərsekolah]
to go to school	**ke sekolah**	[ke sekolah]
alphabet	**alfabet, abjad**	[alfabet], [abdʒ'ad]
subject (at school)	**subjek, mata pelajaran**	[subdʒ'ek], [mata peladʒ'aran]
classroom	**ruang kelas**	[ruaŋ kelas]
lesson	**pelajaran**	[peladʒ'aran]
playtime, break	**waktu istirahat**	[waktu istirahat]
school bell	**lonceng**	[lontʃeŋ]
school desk	**bangku sekolah**	[baŋku sekolah]
blackboard	**papan tulis hitam**	[papan tulis hitam]
mark	**nilai**	[nilaj]
good mark	**nilai baik**	[nilaj baj']
bad mark	**nilai jelek**	[nilaj dʒ'ele']
to give a mark	**memberikan nilai**	[memberikan nilaj]
mistake, error	**kesalahan**	[kesalahan]
to make mistakes	**melakukan kesalahan**	[melakukan kesalahan]
to correct (an error)	**mengoreksi**	[məŋoreksi]
crib	**contekan**	[tʃontekan]
homework	**pekerjaan rumah**	[pekerdʒ'a'an rumah]
exercise (in education)	**latihan**	[latihan]
to be present	**hadir**	[hadir]
to be absent	**absen, tidak hadir**	[absen], [tida' hadir]
to miss school	**absen dari sekolah**	[absen dari sekolah]
to punish (vt)	**menghukum**	[məŋhukum]
punishment	**hukuman**	[hukuman]
conduct (behaviour)	**perilaku**	[pərilaku]

school report	rapor	[rapor]
pencil	pensil	[pensil]
rubber	karet penghapus	[karet peŋhapus]
chalk	kapur	[kapur]
pencil case	kotak pensil	[kota' pensil]

schoolbag	tas sekolah	[tas sekolah]
pen	pen	[pen]
exercise book	buku tulis	[buku tulis]
textbook	buku pelajaran	[buku peladʒʲaran]
compasses	paser, jangka	[paser], [dʒʲaŋka]

| to make technical drawings | menggambar | [məŋgambar] |
| technical drawing | gambar teknik | [gambar tekni'] |

poem	puisi, sajak	[puisi], [sadʒʲa']
by heart (adv)	hafal	[hafal]
to learn by heart	menghafalkan	[məŋhafalkan]

school holidays	liburan sekolah	[liburan sekolah]
to be on holiday	berlibur	[bərlibur]
to spend holidays	menjalani liburan	[məndʒʲalani liburan]

test (at school)	tes, kuis	[tes], [kuis]
essay (composition)	esai, karangan	[esaj], [karaŋan]
dictation	dikte	[dikte]
exam (examination)	ujian	[udʒian]
to do an exam	menempuh ujian	[mənempuh udʒian]
experiment (e.g., chemistry ~)	eksperimen	[eksperimen]

118. College. University

academy	akademi	[akademi]
university	universitas	[universitas]
faculty (e.g., ~ of Medicine)	fakultas	[fakultas]

student (masc.)	mahasiswa	[mahasiswa]
student (fem.)	mahasiswi	[mahasiswi]
lecturer (teacher)	dosen	[dosen]

| lecture hall, room | ruang kuliah | [ruaŋ kuliah] |
| graduate | lulusan | [lulusan] |

| diploma | ijazah | [idʒʲazah] |
| dissertation | disertasi | [disertasi] |

| study (report) | penelitian | [penelitian] |
| laboratory | laboratorium | [laboratorium] |

lecture	kuliah	[kuliah]
coursemate	rekan sekuliah	[rekan sekuliah]
scholarship, bursary	beasiswa	[beasiswa]
academic degree	gelar akademik	[gelar akademi']

119. Sciences. Disciplines

mathematics	matematika	[matematika]
algebra	aljabar	[aldʒʲabar]
geometry	geometri	[geometri]
astronomy	astronomi	[astronomi]
biology	biologi	[biologi]
geography	geografi	[geografi]
geology	geologi	[geologi]
history	sejarah	[sedʒʲarah]
medicine	kedokteran	[kedokteran]
pedagogy	pedagogi	[pedagogi]
law	hukum	[hukum]
physics	fisika	[fisika]
chemistry	kimia	[kimia]
philosophy	filsafat	[filsafat]
psychology	psikologi	[psikologi]

120. Writing system. Orthography

grammar	tatabahasa	[tatabahasa]
vocabulary	kosakata	[kosakata]
phonetics	fonetik	[foneti']
noun	nomina	[nomina]
adjective	adjektiva	[adʒʲektiva]
verb	verba	[verba]
adverb	adverbia	[adverbia]
pronoun	kata ganti	[kata ganti]
interjection	kata seru	[kata seru]
preposition	preposisi, kata depan	[preposisi], [kata depan]
root	kata dasar	[kata dasar]
ending	akhiran	[ahiran]
prefix	prefiks, awalan	[prefiks], [awalan]
syllable	suku kata	[suku kata]
suffix	sufiks, akhiran	[sufiks], [ahiran]
stress mark	tanda tekanan	[tanda tekanan]
apostrophe	apostrofi	[apostrofi]
full stop	titik	[titi']
comma	koma	[koma]
semicolon	titik koma	[titi' koma]
colon	titik dua	[titi' dua]
ellipsis	elipsis, lesapan	[elipsis], [lesapan]
question mark	tanda tanya	[tanda tanja]
exclamation mark	tanda seru	[tanda seru]

inverted commas	tanda petik	[tanda peti']
in inverted commas	dalam tanda petik	[dalam tanda peti']
parenthesis	tanda kurung	[tanda kuruŋ]
in parenthesis	dalam tanda kurung	[dalam tanda kuruŋ]

hyphen	tanda pisah	[tanda pisah]
dash	tanda hubung	[tanda hubuŋ]
space (between words)	spasi	[spasi]

| letter | huruf | [huruf] |
| capital letter | huruf kapital | [huruf kapital] |

| vowel (n) | vokal | [vokal] |
| consonant (n) | konsonan | [konsonan] |

sentence	kalimat	[kalimat]
subject	subjek	[subdʒ'e']
predicate	predikat	[predikat]

line	baris	[baris]
on a new line	di baris baru	[di baris baru]
paragraph	alinea, paragraf	[alinea], [paragraf]

word	kata	[kata]
group of words	rangkaian kata	[raŋkajan kata]
expression	ungkapan	[uŋkapan]
synonym	sinonim	[sinonim]
antonym	antonim	[antonim]

rule	peraturan	[pəraturan]
exception	perkecualian	[pərketʃualian]
correct (adj)	benar, betul	[benar], [betul]

conjugation	konjugasi	[kondʒ'ugasi]
declension	deklinasi	[deklinasi]
nominal case	kasus nominal	[kasus nominal]
question	pertanyaan	[pərtanja'an]
to underline (vt)	menggaris bawahi	[məŋgaris bawahi]
dotted line	garis bertitik	[garis bərtiti']

121. Foreign languages

language	bahasa	[bahasa]
foreign (adj)	asing	[asiŋ]
foreign language	bahasa asing	[bahasa asiŋ]
to study (vt)	mempelajari	[mempeladʒ'ari]
to learn (language, etc.)	belajar	[beladʒ'ar]

to read (vi, vt)	membaca	[membatʃa]
to speak (vi, vt)	berbicara	[bərbitʃara]
to understand (vt)	mengerti	[məŋerti]
to write (vt)	menulis	[mənulis]
fast (adv)	cepat, fasih	[tʃepat], [fasih]
slowly (adv)	perlahan-lahan	[pərlahan-lahan]

fluently (adv)	fasih	[fasih]
rules	peraturan	[pəraturan]
grammar	tatabahasa	[tatabahasa]
vocabulary	kosakata	[kosakata]
phonetics	fonetik	[fonetiʔ]

textbook	buku pelajaran	[buku peladʒʲaran]
dictionary	kamus	[kamus]
teach-yourself book	buku autodidak	[buku autodidaʔ]
phrasebook	panduan percakapan	[panduan pərʧakapan]

cassette, tape	kaset	[kaset]
videotape	kaset video	[kaset video]
CD, compact disc	cakram kompak	[ʧakram kompaʔ]
DVD	cakram DVD	[ʧakram di-vi-di]

alphabet	alfabet, abjad	[alfabet], [abdʒʲad]
to spell (vt)	mengeja	[məŋedʒʲa]
pronunciation	pelafalan	[pelafalan]

accent	aksen	[aksen]
with an accent	dengan aksen	[deŋan aksen]
without an accent	tanpa aksen	[tanpa aksen]

| word | kata | [kata] |
| meaning | arti | [arti] |

course (e.g. a French ~)	kursus	[kursus]
to sign up	Mendaftar	[məndaftar]
teacher	guru	[guru]

translation (process)	penerjemahan	[penerdʒʲemahan]
translation (text, etc.)	terjemahan	[tərdʒʲemahan]
translator	penerjemah	[penerdʒʲemah]
interpreter	juru bahasa	[dʒʲuru bahasa]

| polyglot | poliglot | [poliglot] |
| memory | memori, daya ingat | [memori], [daja iŋat] |

122. Fairy tale characters

Father Christmas	Sinterklas	[sinterklas]
Cinderella	Cinderella	[ʧinderella]
mermaid	putri duyung	[putri duyuŋ]
Neptune	Neptunus	[neptunus]

magician, wizard	penyihir	[penjihir]
fairy	peri	[peri]
magic (adj)	sihir	[sihir]
magic wand	tongkat sihir	[toŋkat sihir]

fairy tale	dongeng	[doŋeŋ]
miracle	keajaiban	[keadʒʲajban]
dwarf	kerdil, katai	[kerdil], [kataj]

to turn into ...	menjelma menjadi ...	[mənʤielma mənʤiadi ...]
ghost	hantu	[hantu]
phantom	fantom	[fantom]
monster	monster	[monster]
dragon	naga	[naga]
giant	raksasa	[raksasa]

123. Zodiac Signs

Aries	**Aries**	[aries]
Taurus	**Taurus**	[taurus]
Gemini	**Gemini**	[ʤiemini]
Cancer	**Cancer**	[kanser]
Leo	**Leo**	[leo]
Virgo	**Virgo**	[virgo]
Libra	**Libra**	[libra]
Scorpio	**Scorpio**	[skorpio]
Sagittarius	**Sagitarius**	[sagitarius]
Capricorn	**Capricorn**	[keprikon]
Aquarius	**Aquarius**	[akuarius]
Pisces	**Pisces**	[pistʃes]
character	**karakter**	[karakter]
character traits	**ciri karakter**	[tʃiri karakter]
behaviour	**tingkah laku**	[tiŋkah laku]
to tell fortunes	**meramal**	[meramal]
fortune-teller	**peramal**	[pəramal]
horoscope	**horoskop**	[horoskop]

Arts

theatre	teater	[teater]
opera	opera	[opera]
operetta	opereta	[opereta]
ballet	balet	[balet]
theatre poster	poster	[poster]
theatre company	rombongan teater	[romboŋan teater]
tour	tur, pertunjukan keliling	[tur], [pərtundʒˈukan keliliŋ]
to be on tour	mengadakan tur	[məŋadakan tur]
to rehearse (vi, vt)	berlatih	[bərlatih]
rehearsal	geladi	[geladi]
repertoire	repertoar	[repertoar]
performance	pertunjukan	[pərtundʒˈukan]
theatrical show	pergelaran	[pərgelaran]
play	lakon	[lakon]
ticket	tiket	[tiket]
booking office	loket tiket	[loket tiket]
lobby, foyer	lobi, ruang depan	[lobi], [ruaŋ depan]
coat check (cloakroom)	tempat penitipan jas	[tempat penitipan dʒˈas]
cloakroom ticket	nomor penitipan jas	[nomor penitipan dʒˈas]
binoculars	binokular	[binokular]
usher	petugas penyobek tiket	[petugas penjobeʔ tiket]
stalls (orchestra seats)	kursi orkestra	[kursi orkestra]
balcony	balkon	[balkon]
dress circle	tingkat pertama	[tiŋkat pərtama]
box	boks	[boks]
row	barisan	[barisan]
seat	tempat duduk	[tempat duduʔ]
audience	khalayak	[halajaʔ]
spectator	penonton	[penonton]
to clap (vi, vt)	bertepuk tangan	[bərtepuʔ taŋan]
applause	aplaus, tepuk tangan	[aplaus], [tepuʔ taŋan]
ovation	ovasi, tepuk tangan	[ovasi], [tepuʔ taŋan]
stage	panggung	[paŋguŋ]
curtain	tirai	[tiraj]
scenery	tata panggung	[tata paŋguŋ]
backstage	belakang panggung	[belakaŋ paŋguŋ]
scene (e.g. the last ~)	adegan	[adegan]
act	babak	[babaʔ]
interval	waktu istirahat	[waktu istirahat]

125. Cinema

actor	**aktor**	[aktor]
actress	**aktris**	[aktris]
cinema (industry)	**sinematografi, perfilman**	[sinematografi], [perfilman]
film	**film**	[film]
episode	**episode, seri**	[episode], [seri]
detective film	**detektif**	[detektif]
action film	**film laga**	[film laga]
adventure film	**film petualangan**	[film petualaŋan]
science fiction film	**film fiksi ilmiah**	[film fiksi ilmiah]
horror film	**film horor**	[film horor]
comedy film	**film komedi**	[film komedi]
melodrama	**melodrama**	[melodrama]
drama	**drama**	[drama]
fictional film	**film fiksi**	[film fiksi]
documentary	**film dokumenter**	[film dokumenter]
cartoon	**kartun**	[kartun]
silent films	**film bisu**	[film bisu]
role (part)	**peran**	[peran]
leading role	**peran utama**	[peran utama]
to play (vi, vt)	**berperan**	[berperan]
film star	**bintang film**	[bintaŋ film]
well-known (adj)	**terkenal**	[terkenal]
famous (adj)	**terkenal**	[terkenal]
popular (adj)	**populer, terkenal**	[populer], [terkenal]
script (screenplay)	**skenario**	[skenario]
scriptwriter	**penulis skenario**	[penulis skenario]
film director	**sutradara**	[sutradara]
producer	**produser**	[produser]
assistant	**asisten**	[asisten]
cameraman	**kamerawan**	[kamerawan]
stuntman	**pemeran pengganti**	[pemeran peŋganti]
double (body double)	**pengganti**	[peŋganti]
to shoot a film	**merekam film**	[merekam film]
audition, screen test	**audisi**	[audisi]
shooting	**syuting, pengambilan gambar**	[ʃyutiŋ], [peŋambilan gambar]
film crew	**rombongan film**	[romboŋan film]
film set	**set film**	[set film]
camera	**kamera**	[kamera]
cinema	**bioskop**	[bioskop]
screen (e.g. big ~)	**layar**	[lajar]
to show a film	**menayangkan film**	[menajaŋkan film]
soundtrack	**soundtrack, trek suara**	[saundtrek], [tre' suara]
special effects	**efek khusus**	[efe' husus]

subtitles	subjudul, teks film	[subdʒiudul], [teks film]
credits	ucapan terima kasih	[utʃapan tərima kasih]
translation	terjemahan	[tərdʒiemahan]

126. Painting

art	seni	[seni]
fine arts	seni rupa	[seni rupa]
art gallery	galeri seni	[galeri seni]
art exhibition	pameran seni	[pameran seni]

painting (art)	seni lukis	[seni lukis]
graphic art	seni grafis	[seni grafis]
abstract art	seni abstrak	[seni abstraʔ]
impressionism	impresionisme	[impresionisme]

picture (painting)	lukisan	[lukisan]
drawing	gambar	[gambar]
poster	poster	[poster]

illustration (picture)	ilustrasi	[ilustrasi]
miniature	miniatur	[miniatur]
copy (of painting, etc.)	salinan	[salinan]
reproduction	reproduksi	[reproduksi]

mosaic	mozaik	[mozajʔ]
stained glass window	kaca berwarna	[katʃa bərwarna]
fresco	fresko	[fresko]
engraving	gravir	[gravir]

bust (sculpture)	patung sedada	[patuŋ sedada]
sculpture	seni patung	[seni patuŋ]
statue	patung	[patuŋ]
plaster of Paris	gips	[gips]
plaster (as adj)	dari gips	[dari gips]

portrait	potret	[potret]
self-portrait	potret diri	[potret diri]
landscape painting	lukisan lanskap	[lukisan lanskap]
still life	alam benda	[alam benda]
caricature	karikatur	[karikatur]
sketch	sketsa	[sketsa]

paint	cat	[tʃat]
watercolor paint	cat air	[tʃat air]
oil (paint)	cat minyak	[tʃat minjaʔ]
pencil	pensil	[pensil]
Indian ink	tinta gambar	[tinta gambar]
charcoal	arang	[araŋ]

to draw (vi, vt)	menggambar	[məŋgambar]
to paint (vi, vt)	melukis	[melukis]
to pose (vi)	berpose	[bərpose]
artist's model (masc.)	model lelaki	[model lelaki]

artist's model (fem.)	model perempuan	[model pərempuan]
artist (painter)	perupa	[pərupa]
work of art	karya seni	[karja seni]
masterpiece	adikarya, mahakarya	[adikarja], [mahakarja]
studio (artist's workroom)	studio seni	[studio seni]
canvas (cloth)	kanvas	[kanvas]
easel	esel, kuda-kuda	[esel], [kuda-kuda]
palette	palet	[palet]
frame (picture ~, etc.)	bingkai	[biŋkaj]
restoration	pemugaran	[pemugaran]
to restore (vt)	memugar	[memugar]

127. Literature & Poetry

literature	sastra, kesusastraan	[sastra], [kesusastraʔan]
author (writer)	pengarang	[peŋaraŋ]
pseudonym	pseudonim, nama samaran	[pseudonim], [nama samaran]
book	buku	[buku]
volume	jilid	[dʒilid]
table of contents	daftar isi	[daftar isi]
page	halaman	[halaman]
main character	karakter utama	[karakter utama]
autograph	tanda tangan	[tanda taŋan]
short story	cerpen	[tʃerpen]
story (novella)	novel, cerita	[novel], [tʃerita]
novel	novel	[novel]
work (writing)	karya	[karja]
fable	fabel	[fabel]
detective novel	novel detektif	[novel detektif]
poem (verse)	puisi, sajak	[puisi], [sadʒ'aʔ]
poetry	puisi	[puisi]
poem (epic, ballad)	puisi	[puisi]
poet	penyair	[penjajr]
fiction	fiksi	[fiksi]
science fiction	fiksi ilmiah	[fiksi ilmiah]
adventures	petualangan	[petualaŋan]
educational literature	literatur pendidikan	[literatur pendidikan]
children's literature	sastra kanak-kanak	[sastra kanaʔ-kanaʔ]

128. Circus

circus	sirkus	[sirkus]
travelling circus	sirkus keliling	[sirkus keliliŋ]
programme	program	[program]
performance	pertunjukan	[pertundʒ'ukan]

act (circus ~)	**aksi**	[aksi]
circus ring	**arena**	[arena]
pantomime (act)	**pantomim**	[pantomim]
clown	**badut**	[badut]
acrobat	**pemain akrobat**	[pemajn akrobat]
acrobatics	**akrobatik**	[akrobatiʔ]
gymnast	**pesenam**	[pesenam]
acrobatic gymnastics	**senam**	[senam]
somersault	**salto**	[salto]
strongman	**orang kuat**	[oraŋ kuat]
tamer (e.g., lion ~)	**penjinak hewan**	[pendʒinaʔ hewan]
rider (circus horse ~)	**penunggang kuda**	[penuŋgaŋ kuda]
assistant	**asisten**	[asisten]
stunt	**stunt**	[stun]
magic trick	**trik sulap**	[triʔ sulap]
conjurer, magician	**pesulap**	[pesulap]
juggler	**juggler**	[dʒⁱuggler]
to juggle (vi, vt)	**bermain juggling**	[bərmajn dʒⁱuggliŋ]
animal trainer	**pelatih binatang**	[pelatih binataŋ]
animal training	**pelatihan binatang**	[pelatihan binataŋ]
to train (animals)	**melatih**	[melatih]

129. Music. Pop music

music	**musik**	[musiʔ]
musician	**musisi, musikus**	[musisi], [musikus]
musical instrument	**alat musik**	[alat musiʔ]
to play …	**bermain …**	[bərmajn …]
guitar	**gitar**	[gitar]
violin	**biola**	[biola]
cello	**selo**	[selo]
double bass	**kontrabas**	[kontrabas]
harp	**harpa**	[harpa]
piano	**piano**	[piano]
grand piano	**grand piano**	[grand piano]
organ	**organ**	[organ]
wind instruments	**alat musik tiup**	[alat musiʔ tiup]
oboe	**obo**	[obo]
saxophone	**saksofon**	[saksofon]
clarinet	**klarinet**	[klarinet]
flute	**suling**	[suliŋ]
trumpet	**trompet**	[trompet]
accordion	**akordeon**	[akordeon]
drum	**drum**	[drum]
duo	**duo, duet**	[duo], [duet]

trio	**trio**	[trio]
quartet	**kuartet**	[kuartet]
choir	**kor**	[kor]
orchestra	**orkestra**	[orkestra]
pop music	**musik pop**	[musiʔ pop]
rock music	**musik rok**	[musiʔ roʔ]
rock group	**grup musik rok**	[grup musiʔ roʔ]
jazz	**jaz**	[dʒˈaz]
idol	**idola**	[idola]
admirer, fan	**pengagum**	[peŋagum]
concert	**konser**	[konser]
symphony	**simfoni**	[simfoni]
composition	**komposisi**	[komposisi]
to compose (write)	**menggubah, mencipta**	[meŋgubah], [mentʃipta]
singing (n)	**nyanyian**	[njanjian]
song	**lagu**	[lagu]
tune (melody)	**nada, melodi**	[nada], [melodi]
rhythm	**irama**	[irama]
blues	**musik blues**	[musiʔ blus]
sheet music	**notasi musik**	[notasi musiʔ]
baton	**tongkat dirigen**	[toŋkat dirigen]
bow	**penggesek**	[peŋgeseʔ]
string	**tali, senar**	[tali], [senar]
case (e.g. guitar ~)	**wadah**	[wadah]

Rest. Entertainment. Travel

130. Trip. Travel

tourism, travel	**pariwisata**	[pariwisata]
tourist	**turis, wisatawan**	[turis], [wisatawan]
trip, voyage	**pengembaraan**	[peɲembara'an]
adventure	**petualangan**	[petualaŋan]
trip, journey	**perjalanan, lawatan**	[pərdʒ'alanan], [lawatan]
holiday	**liburan**	[liburan]
to be on holiday	**berlibur**	[bərlibur]
rest	**istirahat**	[istirahat]
train	**kereta api**	[kereta api]
by train	**naik kereta api**	[nai' kereta api]
aeroplane	**pesawat terbang**	[pesawat tərbaŋ]
by aeroplane	**naik pesawat terbang**	[nai' pesawat tərbaŋ]
by car	**naik mobil**	[nai' mobil]
by ship	**naik kapal**	[nai' kapal]
luggage	**bagasi**	[bagasi]
suitcase	**koper**	[koper]
luggage trolley	**troli bagasi**	[troli bagasi]
passport	**paspor**	[paspor]
visa	**visa**	[visa]
ticket	**tiket**	[tiket]
air ticket	**tiket pesawat terbang**	[tiket pesawat tərbaŋ]
guidebook	**buku pedoman**	[buku pedoman]
map (tourist ~)	**peta**	[peta]
area (rural ~)	**kawasan**	[kawasan]
place, site	**tempat**	[tempat]
exotica (n)	**keeksotisan**	[keeksotisan]
exotic (adj)	**eksotis**	[eksotis]
amazing (adj)	**menakjubkan**	[mənakdʒ'ubkan]
group	**kelompok**	[kelompo']
excursion, sightseeing tour	**ekskursi**	[ekskursi]
guide (person)	**pemandu wisata**	[pemandu wisata]

131. Hotel

hotel	**hotel**	[hotel]
motel	**motel**	[motel]
three-star (~ hotel)	**bintang tiga**	[bintaŋ tiga]

five-star	**bintang lima**	[bintaŋ lima]
to stay (in a hotel, etc.)	**menginap**	[məŋinap]
room	**kamar**	[kamar]
single room	**kamar tunggal**	[kamar tuŋgal]
double room	**kamar ganda**	[kamar ganda]
to book a room	**memesan kamar**	[memesan kamar]
half board	**sewa setengah**	[sewa seteŋah]
full board	**sewa penuh**	[sewa penuh]
with bath	**dengan kamar mandi**	[deŋan kamar mandi]
with shower	**dengan pancuran**	[deŋan panʧuran]
satellite television	**televisi satelit**	[televisi satelit]
air-conditioner	**penyejuk udara**	[penjedʒ'u' udara]
towel	**handuk**	[handu']
key	**kunci**	[kunʧi]
administrator	**administrator**	[administrator]
chambermaid	**pelayan kamar**	[pelajan kamar]
porter	**porter**	[porter]
doorman	**pramupintu**	[pramupintu]
restaurant	**restoran**	[restoran]
pub, bar	**bar**	[bar]
breakfast	**makan pagi, sarapan**	[makan pagi], [sarapan]
dinner	**makan malam**	[makan malam]
buffet	**prasmanan**	[prasmanan]
lobby	**lobi**	[lobi]
lift	**elevator**	[elevator]
DO NOT DISTURB	**JANGAN MENGGANGGU**	[dʒ'aŋan məŋgaŋgu]
NO SMOKING	**DILARANG MEROKOK!**	[dilaraŋ meroko'!]

132. Books. Reading

book	**buku**	[buku]
author	**pengarang**	[peŋaraŋ]
writer	**penulis**	[penulis]
to write (~ a book)	**menulis**	[mənulis]
reader	**pembaca**	[pembaʧa]
to read (vi, vt)	**membaca**	[membaʧa]
reading (activity)	**membaca**	[membaʧa]
silently (to oneself)	**dalam hati**	[dalam hati]
aloud (adv)	**dengan keras**	[deŋan keras]
to publish (vt)	**menerbitkan**	[mənerbitkan]
publishing (process)	**penerbitan**	[penerbitan]
publisher	**penerbit**	[penerbit]
publishing house	**penerbit**	[penerbit]
to come out (be released)	**terbit**	[terbit]

| release (of a book) | penerbitan | [penerbitan] |
| print run | oplah | [oplah] |

| bookshop | toko buku | [toko buku] |
| library | perpustakaan | [pərpustaka'an] |

story (novella)	novel, cerita	[novel], [tʃerita]
short story	cerpen	[tʃerpen]
novel	novel	[novel]
detective novel	novel detektif	[novel detektif]

memoirs	memoir	[memoir]
legend	legenda	[legenda]
myth	mitos	[mitos]

poetry, poems	puisi	[puisi]
autobiography	autobiografi	[autobiografi]
selected works	karya pilihan	[karja pilihan]
science fiction	fiksi ilmiah	[fiksi ilmiah]

title	judul	[dʒiudul]
introduction	pendahuluan	[pendahuluan]
title page	halaman judul	[halaman dʒiudul]

chapter	bab	[bab]
extract	kutipan	[kutipan]
episode	episode	[episode]

plot (storyline)	alur cerita	[alur tʃerita]
contents	daftar isi	[daftar isi]
table of contents	daftar isi	[daftar isi]
main character	karakter utama	[karakter utama]

volume	jilid	[dʒilid]
cover	sampul	[sampul]
binding	penjilidan	[pendʒilidan]
bookmark	pembatas buku	[pembatas buku]

page	halaman	[halaman]
to page through	membolak-balik	[membola'-bali']
margins	margin	[margin]
annotation	anotasi, catatan	[anotasi], [tʃatatan]
(marginal note, etc.)		
footnote	catatan kaki	[tʃatatan kaki]

text	teks	[teks]
type, fount	huruf	[huruf]
misprint, typo	salah cetak	[salah tʃeta']

translation	terjemahan	[tərdʒiemahan]
to translate (vt)	menerjemahkan	[mənərdʒiemahkan]
original (n)	orisinal	[orisinal]

famous (adj)	terkenal	[tərkenal]
unknown (not famous)	tidak dikenali	[tida' dikenali]
interesting (adj)	menarik	[mənari']

bestseller	buku laris	[buku laris]
dictionary	kamus	[kamus]
textbook	buku pelajaran	[buku peladʒɨaran]
encyclopedia	ensiklopedi	[ensiklopedi]

133. Hunting. Fishing

hunting	perburuan	[pərburuan]
to hunt (vi, vt)	berburu	[bərburu]
hunter	pemburu	[pemburu]

to shoot (vi)	menembak	[mənembaʔ]
rifle	senapan	[senapan]
bullet (shell)	peluru, patrun	[peluru], [patrun]
shot (lead balls)	peluru gotri	[peluru gotri]

steel trap	perangkap	[pəraŋkap]
snare (for birds, etc.)	perangkap	[pəraŋkap]
to fall into the steel trap	terperangkap	[tərperaŋkap]
to lay a steel trap	memasang perangkap	[memasaŋ pəraŋkap]

poacher	pemburu ilegal	[pemburu ilegal]
game (in hunting)	binatang buruan	[binataŋ buruan]
hound dog	anjing pemburu	[andʒiŋ pemburu]
safari	safari	[safari]
mounted animal	patung binatang	[patuŋ binataŋ]

fisherman	nelayan, pemancing	[nelajan], [pemantʃiŋ]
fishing (angling)	memancing	[memantʃiŋ]
to fish (vi)	memancing	[memantʃiŋ]

fishing rod	joran	[dʒoran]
fishing line	tali pancing	[tali pantʃiŋ]
hook	kail	[kail]
float	pelampung	[pelampuŋ]
bait	umpan	[umpan]

| to cast a line | melempar pancing | [melempar pantʃiŋ] |
| to bite (ab. fish) | memakan umpan | [memakan umpan] |

| catch (of fish) | tangkapan | [taŋkapan] |
| ice-hole | lubang es | [lubaŋ es] |

fishing net	jala	[dʒɨala]
boat	perahu	[pərahu]
to net (to fish with a net)	menjala	[məndʒɨala]
to cast[throw] the net	menabur jala	[mənabur dʒɨala]

| to haul the net in | menarik jala | [mənariʔ dʒɨala] |
| to fall into the net | tertangkap dalam jala | [tərtaŋkap dalam dʒɨala] |

whaler (person)	pemburu paus	[pemburu paus]
whaleboat	kapal pemburu paus	[kapal pemburu paus]
harpoon	tempuling	[tempuliŋ]

134. Games. Billiards

billiards	**biliar**	[biliar]
billiard room, hall	**kamar biliar**	[kamar biliar]
ball (snooker, etc.)	**bola**	[bola]
to pocket a ball	**memasukkan bola**	[memasuʔkan bola]
cue	**stik**	[stiʔ]
pocket	**lubang meja biliar**	[lubaŋ medʒ'a biliar]

135. Games. Playing cards

diamonds	**wajik**	[wadʒiʔ]
spades	**sekop**	[sekop]
hearts	**hati**	[hati]
clubs	**keriting**	[keritiŋ]
ace	**as**	[as]
king	**raja**	[radʒ'a]
queen	**ratu**	[ratu]
jack, knave	**jack**	[dʒ'eʔ]
playing card	**kartu permainan**	[kartu pərmajnan]
cards	**kartu**	[kartu]
trump	**truf**	[truf]
pack of cards	**pak kartu**	[paʔ kartu]
point	**poin**	[poin]
to deal (vi, vt)	**membagikan**	[membagikan]
to shuffle (cards)	**mengocok**	[məŋotʃoʔ]
lead, turn (n)	**giliran**	[giliran]
cardsharp	**pemain kartu curang**	[pemajn kartu tʃuraŋ]

136. Rest. Games. Miscellaneous

to stroll (vi, vt)	**berjalan-jalan**	[bərdʒ'alan-dʒ'alan]
stroll (leisurely walk)	**jalan-jalan**	[dʒ'alan-dʒ'alan]
car ride	**perjalanan**	[pərdʒ'alanan]
adventure	**petualangan**	[petualaŋan]
picnic	**piknik**	[pikniʔ]
game (chess, etc.)	**permainan**	[pərmajnan]
player	**pemain**	[pemajn]
game (one ~ of chess)	**partai**	[partaj]
collector (e.g. philatelist)	**kolektor**	[kolektor]
to collect (stamps, etc.)	**mengoleksi**	[məŋoleksi]
collection	**koleksi**	[koleksi]
crossword puzzle	**teka-teki silang**	[teka-teki silaŋ]
racecourse (hippodrome)	**lapangan pacu**	[lapaŋan patʃu]

disco (discotheque)	**diskotik**	[diskoti']
sauna	**sauna**	[sauna]
lottery	**lotre**	[lotre]

camping trip	**darmawisata**	[darmawisata]
camp	**perkemahan**	[pərkemahan]
tent (for camping)	**tenda, kemah**	[tenda], [kemah]
compass	**kompas**	[kompas]
camper	**pewisata alam**	[pewisata alam]

to watch (film, etc.)	**menonton**	[mənonton]
viewer	**penonton**	[penonton]
TV show (TV program)	**acara TV**	[atʃara ti-vi]

137. Photography

| camera (photo) | **kamera** | [kamera] |
| photo, picture | **foto** | [foto] |

photographer	**fotografer**	[fotografer]
photo studio	**studio foto**	[studio foto]
photo album	**album foto**	[album foto]

camera lens	**lensa kamera**	[lensa kamera]
telephoto lens	**lensa telefoto**	[lensa telefoto]
filter	**filter**	[filter]
lens	**lensa**	[lensa]

optics (high-quality ~)	**alat optik**	[alat opti']
diaphragm (aperture)	**diafragma**	[diafragma]
exposure time (shutter speed)	**kecepatan rana**	[ketʃepatan rana]

viewfinder	**jendela pengamat**	[dʒˈendela peŋamat]
digital camera	**kamera digital**	[kamera digital]
tripod	**kakitiga**	[kakitiga]
flash	**blitz**	[blits]

to photograph (vt)	**memotret**	[memotret]
to take pictures	**memotret**	[memotret]
to have one's picture taken	**berfoto**	[bərfoto]

focus	**fokus**	[fokus]
to focus	**mengatur fokus**	[məŋatur fokus]
sharp, in focus (adj)	**tajam**	[tadʒˈam]
sharpness	**ketajaman**	[ketadʒˈaman]

| contrast | **kekontrasan** | [kekontrasan] |
| contrast (as adj) | **kontras** | [kontras] |

picture (photo)	**gambar foto**	[gambar foto]
negative (n)	**negatif**	[negatif]
film (a roll of ~)	**film**	[film]
frame (still)	**frame, gambar diam**	[frame], [gambar diam]
to print (photos)	**mencetak**	[məntʃeta']

138. Beach. Swimming

beach	**pantai**	[pantaj]
sand	**pasir**	[pasir]
deserted (beach)	**sepi**	[sepi]
suntan	**hitam terbakar matahari**	[hitam tərbakar matahari]
to get a tan	**berjemur di sinar matahari**	[bərdʒ'emur di sinar matahari]
tanned (adj)	**hitam terbakar matahari**	[hitam tərbakar matahari]
sunscreen	**tabir surya**	[tabir surja]
bikini	**bikini**	[bikini]
swimsuit, bikini	**baju renang**	[badʒ'u renaŋ]
swim trunks	**celana renang**	[tʃelana renaŋ]
swimming pool	**kolam renang**	[kolam renaŋ]
to swim (vi)	**berenang**	[bərenaŋ]
shower	**pancuran**	[pantʃuran]
to change (one's clothes)	**berganti pakaian**	[bərganti pakajan]
towel	**handuk**	[handu']
boat	**perahu**	[pərahu]
motorboat	**perahu motor**	[pərahu motor]
water ski	**ski air**	[ski air]
pedalo	**sepeda air**	[sepeda air]
surfing	**berselancar**	[bərselantʃar]
surfer	**peselancar**	[peselantʃar]
scuba set	**alat scuba**	[alat skuba]
flippers (swim fins)	**sirip karet**	[sirip karet]
mask (diving ~)	**masker**	[masker]
diver	**penyelam**	[penjelam]
to dive (vi)	**menyelam**	[mənjelam]
underwater (adv)	**bawah air**	[bawah air]
beach umbrella	**payung**	[pajuŋ]
beach chair (sun lounger)	**kursi pantai**	[kursi pantaj]
sunglasses	**kacamata hitam**	[katʃamata hitam]
air mattress	**kasur udara**	[kasur udara]
to play (amuse oneself)	**bermain**	[bərmajn]
to go for a swim	**berenang**	[bərenaŋ]
beach ball	**bola pantai**	[bola pantaj]
to inflate (vt)	**meniup**	[məniup]
inflatable, air (adj)	**udara**	[udara]
wave	**gelombang**	[gelombaŋ]
buoy (line of ~s)	**pelampung**	[pelampuŋ]
to drown (ab. person)	**tenggelam**	[teŋgelam]
to save, to rescue	**menyelamatkan**	[mənjelamatkan]
life jacket	**jaket pelampung**	[dʒ'aket pelampuŋ]
to observe, to watch	**mengamati**	[məŋamati]
lifeguard	**penyelamat**	[penjelamat]

TECHNICAL EQUIPMENT. TRANSPORT

Technical equipment

139. Computer

computer	**komputer**	[komputer]
notebook, laptop	**laptop**	[laptop]
to turn on	**menyalakan**	[mənjalakan]
to turn off	**mematikan**	[mematikan]
keyboard	**keyboard, papan tombol**	[keybor], [papan tombol]
key	**tombol**	[tombol]
mouse	**tetikus**	[tetikus]
mouse mat	**bantal tetikus**	[bantal tetikus]
button	**tombol**	[tombol]
cursor	**kursor**	[kursor]
monitor	**monitor**	[monitor]
screen	**layar**	[lajar]
hard disk	**hard disk, cakram keras**	[hard disk], [tʃakram keras]
hard disk capacity	**kapasitas cakram keras**	[kapasitas tʃakram keras]
memory	**memori**	[memori]
random access memory	**memori akses acak**	[memori akses atʃaʔ]
file	**file, berkas**	[file], [bərkas]
folder	**folder**	[folder]
to open (vt)	**membuka**	[membuka]
to close (vt)	**menutup**	[mənutup]
to save (vt)	**menyimpan**	[mənjimpan]
to delete (vt)	**menghapus**	[məŋhapus]
to copy (vt)	**menyalin**	[mənjalin]
to sort (vt)	**menyortir**	[mənjortir]
to transfer (copy)	**mentransfer**	[mentransfer]
programme	**program**	[program]
software	**perangkat lunak**	[pəraŋkat lunaʔ]
programmer	**pemrogram**	[pemrogram]
to program (vt)	**memprogram**	[memprogram]
hacker	**peretas**	[pəretas]
password	**kata sandi**	[kata sandi]
virus	**virus**	[virus]
to find, to detect	**mendeteksi**	[məndeteksi]
byte	**bita**	[bita]

megabyte	megabita	[megabita]
data	data	[data]
database	basis data, pangkalan data	[basis data], [paŋkalan data]

cable (USB, etc.)	kabel	[kabel]
to disconnect (vt)	melepaskan	[melepaskan]
to connect (sth to sth)	menyambungkan	[mənjambuŋkan]

140. Internet. E-mail

Internet	Internet	[internet]
browser	peramban	[pəramban]
search engine	mesin telusur	[mesin telusur]
provider	provider	[provider]

webmaster	webmaster, perancang web	[webmaster], [pərantʃaŋ web]
website	situs web	[situs web]
web page	halaman web	[halaman web]

address (e-mail ~)	alamat	[alamat]
address book	buku alamat	[buku alamat]

postbox	kotak surat	[kota' surat]
post	surat	[surat]
full (adj)	penuh	[penuh]

message	pesan	[pesan]
incoming messages	pesan masuk	[pesan masu']
outgoing messages	pesan keluar	[pesan keluar]

sender	pengirim	[peɲirim]
to send (vt)	mengirim	[məɲirim]
sending (of mail)	pengiriman	[peɲiriman]

receiver	penerima	[penerima]
to receive (vt)	menerima	[mənerima]

correspondence	surat-menyurat	[surat-menyurat]
to correspond (vi)	surat-menyurat	[surat-menyurat]

file	file, berkas	[file], [bərkas]
to download (vt)	mengunduh	[məŋunduh]
to create (vt)	membuat	[membuat]
to delete (vt)	menghapus	[məɲhapus]
deleted (adj)	terhapus	[tərhapus]

connection (ADSL, etc.)	koneksi	[koneksi]
speed	kecepatan	[ketʃepatan]
modem	modem	[modem]
access	akses	[akses]
port (e.g. input ~)	porta	[porta]

connection (make a ~)	koneksi	[koneksi]
to connect to … (vi)	terhubung ke …	[tərhubuŋ ke …]

| to select (vt) | memilih | [memilih] |
| to search (for …) | mencari … | [mənʧari …] |

Transport

aeroplane	**pesawat terbang**	[pesawat tərbaŋ]
air ticket	**tiket pesawat terbang**	[tiket pesawat tərbaŋ]
airline	**maskapai penerbangan**	[maskapaj penerbaŋan]
airport	**bandara**	[bandara]
supersonic (adj)	**supersonik**	[supersoniʔ]
captain	**kapten**	[kapten]
crew	**awak**	[awaʔ]
pilot	**pilot**	[pilot]
stewardess	**pramugari**	[pramugari]
navigator	**navigator, penavigasi**	[navigator], [penavigasi]
wings	**sayap**	[sajap]
tail	**ekor**	[ekor]
cockpit	**kokpit**	[kokpit]
engine	**mesin**	[mesin]
undercarriage (landing gear)	**roda pendarat**	[roda pendarat]
turbine	**turbin**	[turbin]
propeller	**baling-baling**	[baliŋ-baliŋ]
black box	**kotak hitam**	[kota' hitam]
yoke (control column)	**kemudi**	[kemudi]
fuel	**bahan bakar**	[bahan bakar]
safety card	**instruksi keselamatan**	[instruksi keselamatan]
oxygen mask	**masker oksigen**	[masker oksigen]
uniform	**seragam**	[seragam]
lifejacket	**jaket pelampung**	[dʒʲaket pelampuŋ]
parachute	**parasut**	[parasut]
takeoff	**lepas landas**	[lepas landas]
to take off (vi)	**bertolak**	[bərtolaʔ]
runway	**jalur lepas landas**	[dʒʲalur lepas landas]
visibility	**visibilitas, pandangan**	[visibilitas], [pandaŋan]
flight (act of flying)	**penerbangan**	[penerbaŋan]
altitude	**ketinggian**	[ketiŋgian]
air pocket	**lubang udara**	[lubaŋ udara]
seat	**tempat duduk**	[tempat dudu']
headphones	**headphone, fonkepala**	[headphone], [fonkepala]
folding tray (tray table)	**meja lipat**	[medʒʲa lipat]
airplane window	**jendela pesawat**	[dʒʲendela pesawat]
aisle	**lorong**	[loroŋ]

142. Train

train	kereta api	[kereta api]
commuter train	kereta api listrik	[kereta api listri']
express train	kereta api cepat	[kereta api tʃepat]
diesel locomotive	lokomotif diesel	[lokomotif disel]
steam locomotive	lokomotif uap	[lokomotif uap]
coach, carriage	gerbong penumpang	[gerboŋ penumpaŋ]
buffet car	gerbong makan	[gerboŋ makan]
rails	rel	[rel]
railway	rel kereta api	[rel kereta api]
sleeper (track support)	bantalan rel	[bantalan rel]
platform (railway ~)	platform	[platform]
platform (~ 1, 2, etc.)	jalur	[dʒ'alur]
semaphore	semafor	[semafor]
station	stasiun	[stasiun]
train driver	masinis	[masinis]
porter (of luggage)	porter	[porter]
carriage attendant	kondektur	[kondektur]
passenger	penumpang	[penumpaŋ]
ticket inspector	kondektur	[kondektur]
corridor (in train)	koridor	[koridor]
emergency brake	rem darurat	[rem darurat]
compartment	kabin	[kabin]
berth	bangku	[baŋku]
upper berth	bangku atas	[baŋku atas]
lower berth	bangku bawah	[baŋku bawah]
bed linen, bedding	kain kasur	[kain kasur]
ticket	tiket	[tiket]
timetable	jadwal	[dʒ'adwal]
information display	layar informasi	[lajar informasi]
to leave, to depart	berangkat	[bəraŋkat]
departure (of a train)	keberangkatan	[kebəraŋkatan]
to arrive (ab. train)	datang	[dataŋ]
arrival	kedatangan	[kedataŋan]
to arrive by train	datang naik kereta api	[dataŋ naj' kereta api]
to get on the train	naik ke kereta	[nai' ke kereta]
to get off the train	turun dari kereta	[turun dari kereta]
train crash	kecelakaan kereta	[ketʃelaka'an kereta]
to derail (vi)	keluar rel	[keluar rel]
steam locomotive	lokomotif uap	[lokomotif uap]
stoker, fireman	juru api	[dʒ'uru api]
firebox	tungku	[tuŋku]
coal	batu bara	[batu bara]

143. Ship

ship	**kapal**	[kapal]
vessel	**kapal**	[kapal]
steamship	**kapal uap**	[kapal uap]
riverboat	**kapal api**	[kapal api]
cruise ship	**kapal laut**	[kapal laut]
cruiser	**kapal penjelajah**	[kapal pendʒ'eladʒ'ah]
yacht	**perahu pesiar**	[pərahu pesiar]
tugboat	**kapal tunda**	[kapal tunda]
barge	**tongkang**	[toŋkaŋ]
ferry	**feri**	[feri]
sailing ship	**kapal layar**	[kapal lajar]
brigantine	**kapal brigantin**	[kapal brigantin]
ice breaker	**kapal pemecah es**	[kapal pemetʃah es]
submarine	**kapal selam**	[kapal selam]
boat (flat-bottomed ~)	**perahu**	[pərahu]
dinghy (lifeboat)	**sekoci**	[sekotʃi]
lifeboat	**sekoci penyelamat**	[sekotʃi penjelamat]
motorboat	**perahu motor**	[pərahu motor]
captain	**kapten**	[kapten]
seaman	**kelasi**	[kelasi]
sailor	**pelaut**	[pelaut]
crew	**awak**	[awaʔ]
boatswain	**bosman, bosun**	[bosman], [bosun]
ship's boy	**kadet laut**	[kadet laut]
cook	**koki**	[koki]
ship's doctor	**dokter kapal**	[dokter kapal]
deck	**dek**	[deʔ]
mast	**tiang**	[tiaŋ]
sail	**layar**	[lajar]
hold	**lambung kapal**	[lambuŋ kapal]
bow (prow)	**haluan**	[haluan]
stern	**buritan**	[buritan]
oar	**dayung**	[dajuŋ]
screw propeller	**baling-baling**	[baliŋ-baliŋ]
cabin	**kabin**	[kabin]
wardroom	**ruang rekreasi**	[ruaŋ rekreasi]
engine room	**ruang mesin**	[ruaŋ mesin]
bridge	**anjungan kapal**	[andʒ'uŋan kapal]
radio room	**ruang radio**	[ruaŋ radio]
wave (radio)	**gelombang radio**	[gelombaŋ radio]
logbook	**buku harian kapal**	[buku harian kapal]
spyglass	**teropong**	[teropoŋ]
bell	**lonceng**	[lontʃeŋ]

flag	bendera	[bendera]
hawser (mooring ~)	tali	[tali]
knot (bowline, etc.)	simpul	[simpul]

| deckrails | pegangan | [pegaŋan] |
| gangway | tangga kapal | [taŋga kapal] |

anchor	jangkar	[dʒʲaŋkar]
to weigh anchor	mengangkat jangkar	[məŋaŋkat dʒʲaŋkar]
to drop anchor	menjatuhkan jangkar	[məndʒʲatuhkan dʒʲaŋkar]
anchor chain	rantai jangkar	[rantaj dʒʲaŋkar]

port (harbour)	pelabuhan	[pelabuhan]
quay, wharf	dermaga	[dermaga]
to berth (moor)	merapat	[merapat]
to cast off	bertolak	[bərtolaʔ]

trip, voyage	pengembaraan	[peŋembaraʔan]
cruise (sea trip)	pesiar	[pesiar]
course (route)	haluan	[haluan]
route (itinerary)	rute	[rute]

| shallows | beting | [betiŋ] |
| to run aground | kandas | [kandas] |

storm	badai	[badaj]
signal	sinyal	[sinjal]
to sink (vi)	tenggelam	[teŋgelam]
Man overboard!	Orang hanyut!	[oraŋ hanyut!]
SOS (distress signal)	SOS	[es-o-es]
ring buoy	pelampung penyelamat	[pelampuŋ penjelamat]

144. Airport

airport	bandara	[bandara]
aeroplane	pesawat terbang	[pesawat tərbaŋ]
airline	maskapai penerbangan	[maskapaj penerbaŋan]
air traffic controller	pengawas lalu lintas udara	[peŋawas lalu lintas udara]

departure	keberangkatan	[keberaŋkatan]
arrival	kedatangan	[kedataŋan]
to arrive (by plane)	datang	[dataŋ]

| departure time | waktu keberangkatan | [waktu keberaŋkatan] |
| arrival time | waktu kedatangan | [waktu kedataŋan] |

| to be delayed | terlambat | [tərlambat] |
| flight delay | penundaan penerbangan | [penundaʔan penerbaŋan] |

information board	papan informasi	[papan informasi]
information	informasi	[informasi]
to announce (vt)	mengumumkan	[məŋumumkan]
flight (e.g. next ~)	penerbangan	[penerbaŋan]
customs	pabean	[pabean]

customs officer	petugas pabean	[petugas pabean]
customs declaration	pernyataan pabean	[pərnjata'an pabean]
to fill in (vt)	mengisi	[məɲisi]
to fill in the declaration	mengisi formulir bea cukai	[məɲisi formulir bea ʧukaj]
passport control	pemeriksaan paspor	[pemeriksa'an paspor]

luggage	bagasi	[bagasi]
hand luggage	jinjingan	[ʤinʤiŋan]
luggage trolley	troli bagasi	[troli bagasi]

landing	pendaratan	[pendaratan]
landing strip	jalur pendaratan	[ʤ'alur pendaratan]
to land (vi)	mendarat	[məndarat]
airstair (passenger stair)	tangga pesawat	[taŋga pesawat]

check-in	check-in	[ʧekin]
check-in counter	meja check-in	[meʤ'a ʧekin]
to check-in (vi)	check-in	[ʧekin]
boarding card	kartu pas	[kartu pas]
departure gate	gerbang keberangkatan	[gerbaŋ keberaŋkatan]

transit	transit	[transit]
to wait (vt)	menunggu	[mənuŋgu]
departure lounge	ruang tunggu	[ruaŋ tuŋgu]
to see off	mengantar	[məŋantar]
to say goodbye	berpamitan	[bərpamitan]

145. Bicycle. Motorcycle

bicycle	sepeda	[sepeda]
scooter	skuter	[skuter]
motorbike	sepeda motor	[sepeda motor]

to go by bicycle	naik sepeda	[nai' sepeda]
handlebars	kemudi, setang	[kemudi], [setaŋ]
pedal	pedal	[pedal]
brakes	rem	[rem]
bicycle seat (saddle)	sadel	[sadel]

pump	pompa	[pompa]
pannier rack	boncengan	[bonʧeŋan]
front lamp	lampu depan, berko	[lampu depan], [bərko]
helmet	helm	[helm]

wheel	roda	[roda]
mudguard	sayap roda	[sajap roda]
rim	bingkai	[biŋkaj]
spoke	jari-jari, ruji	[ʤ'ari-ʤ'ari], [ruʤi]

Cars

car	**mobil**	[mobil]
sports car	**mobil sports**	[mobil sports]
limousine	**limusin**	[limusin]
off-road vehicle	**kendaraan lintas medan**	[kendaraʔan lintas medan]
drophead coupé (convertible)	**kabriolet**	[kabriolet]
minibus	**minibus**	[minibus]
ambulance	**ambulans**	[ambulans]
snowplough	**truk pembersih salju**	[truʔ pembersih saldʒʲu]
lorry	**truk**	[truʔ]
road tanker	**truk tangki**	[truʔ taŋki]
van (small truck)	**mobil van**	[mobil van]
tractor unit	**truk semi trailer**	[traʔ semi treyler]
trailer	**trailer**	[treyler]
comfortable (adj)	**nyaman**	[njaman]
used (adj)	**bekas**	[bekas]

bonnet	**kap**	[kap]
wing	**sepatbor**	[sepatbor]
roof	**atap**	[atap]
windscreen	**kaca depan**	[katʃa depan]
rear-view mirror	**spion belakang**	[spion belakaŋ]
windscreen washer	**pencuci kaca**	[pentʃutʃi katʃa]
windscreen wipers	**karet wiper**	[karet wiper]
side window	**jendela mobil**	[dʒʲendela mobil]
electric window	**pemutar jendela**	[pemutar dʒʲendela]
aerial	**antena**	[antena]
sunroof	**panel atap**	[panel atap]
bumper	**bumper**	[bumper]
boot	**bagasi mobil**	[bagasi mobil]
roof luggage rack	**rak bagasi atas**	[raʔ bagasi atas]
door	**pintu**	[pintu]
door handle	**gagang pintu**	[gagaŋ pintu]
door lock	**kunci**	[kuntʃi]
number plate	**pelat nomor**	[pelat nomor]
silencer	**peredam suara**	[peredam suara]

petrol tank	**tangki bahan bakar**	[taŋki bahan bakar]
exhaust pipe	**knalpot**	[knalpot]
accelerator	**gas**	[gas]
pedal	**pedal**	[pedal]
accelerator pedal	**pedal gas**	[pedal gas]
brake	**rem**	[rem]
brake pedal	**pedal rem**	[pedal rem]
to brake (use the brake)	**mengerem**	[məŋerem]
handbrake	**rem tangan**	[rem taŋan]
clutch	**kopling**	[kopliŋ]
clutch pedal	**pedal kopling**	[pedal kopliŋ]
clutch disc	**pelat kopling**	[pelat kopliŋ]
shock absorber	**peredam kejut**	[pəredam kedʒʲut]
wheel	**roda**	[roda]
spare tyre	**ban serep**	[ban serep]
tyre	**ban**	[ban]
wheel cover (hubcap)	**dop**	[dop]
driving wheels	**roda penggerak**	[roda peŋgera']
front-wheel drive (as adj)	**penggerak roda depan**	[peŋgera' roda depan]
rear-wheel drive (as adj)	**penggerak roda belakang**	[peŋgera' roda belakaŋ]
all-wheel drive (as adj)	**penggerak roda empat**	[peŋgera' roda empat]
gearbox	**transmisi, girboks**	[transmisi], [girboks]
automatic (adj)	**otomatis**	[otomatis]
mechanical (adj)	**mekanis**	[mekanis]
gear lever	**tuas persneling**	[tuas pərsneliŋ]
headlamp	**lampu depan**	[lampu depan]
headlights	**lampu depan**	[lampu depan]
dipped headlights	**lampu dekat**	[lampu dekat]
full headlights	**lampu jauh**	[lampu dʒʲauh]
brake light	**lampu rem**	[lampu rem]
sidelights	**lampu kecil**	[lampu ketʃil]
hazard lights	**lampu bahaya**	[lampu bahaja]
fog lights	**lampu kabut**	[lampu kabut]
turn indicator	**lampu sein**	[lampu sein]
reversing light	**lampu belakang**	[lampu belakaŋ]

148. Cars. Passenger compartment

car interior	**kabin, interior**	[kabin], [interior]
leather (as adj)	**kulit**	[kulit]
velour (as adj)	**velour**	[velour]
upholstery	**pelapis jok**	[pelapis dʒo']
instrument (gage)	**alat pengukur**	[alat peŋukur]
dashboard	**dasbor**	[dasbor]

| speedometer | **spidometer** | [spidometer] |
| needle (pointer) | **jarum** | [dʒarum] |

mileometer	**odometer**	[odometer]
indicator (sensor)	**indikator, sensor**	[indikator], [sensor]
level	**level**	[level]
warning light	**lampu indikator**	[lampu indikator]

steering wheel	**setir**	[setir]
horn	**klakson**	[klakson]
button	**tombol**	[tombol]
switch	**tuas**	[tuas]

seat	**jok**	[dʒoʔ]
backrest	**sandaran**	[sandaran]
headrest	**sandaran kepala**	[sandaran kepala]
seat belt	**sabuk pengaman**	[sabuʔ peŋaman]
to fasten the belt	**mengencangkan sabuk pengaman**	[məŋentʃaŋkan sabuʔ peŋaman]
adjustment (of seats)	**penyetelan**	[penjetelan]

| airbag | **bantal udara** | [bantal udara] |
| air-conditioner | **penyejuk udara** | [penjedʒuʔ udara] |

radio	**radio**	[radio]
CD player	**pemutar CD**	[pemutar si-di]
to turn on	**menyalakan**	[mənjalakan]
aerial	**antena**	[antena]
glove box	**laci depan**	[latʃi depan]
ashtray	**asbak**	[asbaʔ]

149. Cars. Engine

engine	**mesin**	[mesin]
motor	**motor**	[motor]
diesel (as adj)	**diesel**	[disel]
petrol (as adj)	**bensin**	[bensin]

engine volume	**kapasitas mesin**	[kapasitas mesin]
power	**daya, tenaga**	[daja], [tenaga]
horsepower	**tenaga kuda**	[tenaga kuda]
piston	**piston**	[piston]
cylinder	**silinder**	[silinder]
valve	**katup**	[katup]

injector	**injektor**	[indʒektor]
generator (alternator)	**generator**	[generator]
carburettor	**karburator**	[karburator]
motor oil	**oli**	[oli]

radiator	**radiator**	[radiator]
coolant	**cairan pendingin**	[tʃajran pendiŋin]
cooling fan	**kipas angin**	[kipas aŋin]
battery (accumulator)	**aki**	[aki]

starter	starter	[starter]
ignition	pengapian	[peŋapian]
sparking plug	busi	[busi]

terminal (battery ~)	elektroda	[elektroda]
positive terminal	terminal positif	[terminal positif]
negative terminal	terminal negatif	[terminal negatif]
fuse	sekering	[sekeriŋ]

air filter	filter udara	[filter udara]
oil filter	filter oli	[filter oli]
fuel filter	filter bahan bakar	[filter bahan bakar]

150. Cars. Crash. Repair

car crash	kecelakaan mobil	[ketʃelaka'an mobil]
traffic accident	kecelakaan jalan raya	[ketʃelaka'an dʒ'alan raja]
to crash (into the wall, etc.)	menabrak	[menabra']
to get smashed up	mengalami kecelakaan	[meŋalami ketʃelaka'an]
damage	kerusakan	[kerusakan]
intact (unscathed)	tidak tersentuh	[tida' tersentuh]

breakdown	kerusakan	[kerusakan]
to break down (vi)	rusak	[rusa']
towrope	tali penyeret	[tali penjeret]

puncture	ban bocor	[ban botʃor]
to have a puncture	kempes	[kempes]
to pump up	memompa	[memompa]
pressure	tekanan	[tekanan]
to check (to examine)	memeriksa	[memeriksa]

repair	reparasi	[reparasi]
garage (auto service shop)	bengkel mobil	[beŋkel mobil]
spare part	onderdil, suku cadang	[onderdil], [suku tʃadaŋ]
part	komponen	[komponen]

bolt (with nut)	baut	[baut]
screw (fastener)	sekrup	[sekrup]
nut	mur	[mur]
washer	ring	[riŋ]
bearing (e.g. ball ~)	bantalan luncur	[bantalan luntʃur]

tube	pipa	[pipa]
gasket (head ~)	gasket	[gasket]
cable, wire	kabel, kawat	[kabel], [kawat]

jack	dongkrak	[doŋkra']
spanner	kunci pas	[kuntʃi pas]
hammer	martil, palu	[martil], [palu]
pump	pompa	[pompa]
screwdriver	obeng	[obeŋ]
fire extinguisher	pemadam api	[pemadam api]
warning triangle	segi tiga pengaman	[segi tiga peŋaman]

to stall (vi)	mogok	[mogoˀ]
stall (n)	mogok	[mogoˀ]
to be broken	rusak	[rusaˀ]
to overheat (vi)	kepanasan	[kepanasan]
to be clogged up	tersumbat	[tərsumbat]
to freeze up (pipes, etc.)	membeku	[membeku]
to burst (vi, ab. tube)	pecah	[petʃah]
pressure	tekanan	[tekanan]
level	level	[level]
slack (~ belt)	longgar	[loŋgar]
dent	penyok	[penjoˀ]
knocking noise (engine)	ketukan	[ketukan]
crack	retak	[retaˀ]
scratch	gores	[gores]

151. Cars. Road

road	jalan	[dʒʲalan]
motorway	jalan raya	[dʒʲalan raja]
highway	jalan raya	[dʒʲalan raja]
direction (way)	arah	[arah]
distance	jarak	[dʒʲaraˀ]
bridge	jembatan	[dʒʲembatan]
car park	tempat parkir	[tempat parkir]
square	lapangan	[lapaŋan]
road junction	jembatan simpang susun	[dʒʲembatan simpaŋ susun]
tunnel	terowongan	[tərowoŋan]
petrol station	SPBU, stasiun bensin	[es-pe-be-u], [stasjun bensin]
car park	tempat parkir	[tempat parkir]
petrol pump	stasiun bahan bakar	[stasiun bahan bakar]
auto repair shop	bengkel mobil	[beŋkel mobil]
to fill up	mengisi bahan bakar	[məŋisi bahan bakar]
fuel	bahan bakar	[bahan bakar]
jerrycan	jeriken	[dʒʲeriken]
asphalt, tarmac	aspal	[aspal]
road markings	penandaan jalan	[penandaˀan dʒʲalan]
kerb	kerb jalan	[kerb dʒʲalan]
crash barrier	pagar pematas	[pagar pematas]
ditch	parit	[parit]
roadside (shoulder)	bahu jalan	[bahu dʒʲalan]
lamppost	tiang lampu	[tiaŋ lampu]
to drive (a car)	menyetir	[mənjetir]
to turn (e.g., ~ left)	membelok	[membeloˀ]
to make a U-turn	memutar arah	[memutar arah]
reverse (~ gear)	mundur	[mundur]
to honk (vi)	membunyikan klakson	[membunjikan klakson]
honk (sound)	suara klakson	[suara klakson]

to get stuck (in the mud, etc.)	**terjebak**	[tərdʒ'eba']
to spin the wheels	**terjebak**	[tərdʒ'eba']
to cut, to turn off (vt)	**mematikan**	[mematikan]
speed	**kecepatan**	[ketʃepatan]
to exceed the speed limit	**melebihi batas kecepatan**	[melebihi batas ketʃepatan]
to give a ticket	**memberikan surat tilang**	[memberikan surat tilaŋ]
traffic lights	**lampu lalu lintas**	[lampu lalu lintas]
driving licence	**Surat Izin Mengemudi, SIM**	[surat izin məŋemudi], [sim]
level crossing	**lintasan**	[lintasan]
crossroads	**persimpangan**	[pərsimpaŋan]
zebra crossing	**penyeberangan**	[penjeberaŋan]
bend, curve	**tikungan**	[tikuŋan]
pedestrian precinct	**kawasan pejalan kaki**	[kawasan pedʒ'alan kaki]

PEOPLE. LIFE EVENTS

152. Holidays. Event

celebration, holiday	perayaan	[pəraja'an]
national day	hari besar nasional	[hari besar nasional]
public holiday	hari libur	[hari libur]
to commemorate (vt)	merayakan	[merajakan]
event (happening)	peristiwa, kejadian	[pəristiwa], [kedʒˈadian]
event (organized activity)	acara	[atʃara]
banquet (party)	banket	[banket]
reception (formal party)	resepsi	[resepsi]
feast	pesta	[pesta]
anniversary	hari jadi, HUT	[hari dʒˈadi], [ha-u-te]
jubilee	yubileum	[yubileum]
to celebrate (vt)	merayakan	[merajakan]
New Year	Tahun Baru	[tahun baru]
Happy New Year!	Selamat Tahun Baru!	[selamat tahun baru!]
Father Christmas	Sinterklas	[sinterklas]
Christmas	Natal	[natal]
Merry Christmas!	Selamat Hari Natal!	[selamat hari natal!]
Christmas tree	pohon Natal	[pohon natal]
fireworks (fireworks show)	kembang api	[kembaŋ api]
wedding	pernikahan	[pərnikahan]
groom	mempelai lelaki	[mempelaj lelaki]
bride	mempelai perempuan	[mempelaj pərempuan]
to invite (vt)	mengundang	[məŋundaŋ]
invitation card	kartu undangan	[kartu undaŋan]
guest	tamu	[tamu]
to visit (~ your parents, etc.)	mengunjungi	[məŋundʒˈuŋi]
to meet the guests	menyambut tamu	[mənjambut tamu]
gift, present	hadiah	[hadiah]
to give (sth as present)	memberi	[memberi]
to receive gifts	menerima hadiah	[mənerima hadiah]
bouquet (of flowers)	buket	[buket]
congratulations	ucapan selamat	[utʃapan selamat]
to congratulate (vt)	mengucapkan selamat	[mənutʃapkan selamat]
greetings card	kartu ucapan selamat	[kartu utʃapan selamat]
to send a postcard	mengirim kartu pos	[məŋirim kartu pos]
to get a postcard	menerima kartu pos	[mənerima kartu pos]

toast	**toas**	[toas]
to offer (a drink, etc.)	**menawari**	[mənawari]
champagne	**sampanye**	[sampanje]
to enjoy oneself	**bersukaria**	[bərsukaria]
merriment (gaiety)	**keriangan, kegembiraan**	[keriaŋan], [kegembira'an]
joy (emotion)	**kegembiraan**	[kegembira'an]
dance	**dansa, tari**	[dansa], [tari]
to dance (vi, vt)	**berdansa, menari**	[bərdansa], [menari]
waltz	**wals**	[wals]
tango	**tango**	[taŋo]

153. Funerals. Burial

cemetery	**pemakaman**	[pemakaman]
grave, tomb	**makam**	[makam]
cross	**salib**	[salib]
gravestone	**batu nisan**	[batu nisan]
fence	**pagar**	[pagar]
chapel	**kapel**	[kapel]
death	**kematian**	[kematian]
to die (vi)	**mati, meninggal**	[mati], [meniŋgal]
the deceased	**almarhum**	[almarhum]
mourning	**perkabungan**	[pərkabuŋan]
to bury (vt)	**memakamkan**	[memakamkan]
undertakers	**rumah duka**	[rumah duka]
funeral	**pemakaman**	[pemakaman]
wreath	**karangan bunga**	[karaŋan buŋa]
coffin	**keranda**	[keranda]
hearse	**mobil jenazah**	[mobil dʒʲenazah]
shroud	**kain kafan**	[kain kafan]
funeral procession	**prosesi pemakaman**	[prosesi pemakaman]
funerary urn	**guci abu jenazah**	[gutʃi abu dʒʲenazah]
crematorium	**krematorium**	[krematorium]
obituary	**obituarium**	[obituarium]
to cry (weep)	**menangis**	[mənaŋis]
to sob (vi)	**meratap**	[meratap]

154. War. Soldiers

platoon	**peleton**	[peleton]
company	**kompi**	[kompi]
regiment	**resimen**	[resimen]
army	**tentara**	[tentara]
division	**divisi**	[divisi]

section, squad	**pasukan**	[pasukan]
host (army)	**tentara**	[tentara]
soldier	**tentara, serdadu**	[tentara], [serdadu]
officer	**perwira**	[pərwira]
private	**prajurit**	[pradʒˈurit]
sergeant	**sersan**	[sersan]
lieutenant	**letnan**	[letnan]
captain	**kapten**	[kapten]
major	**mayor**	[major]
colonel	**kolonel**	[kolonel]
general	**jenderal**	[dʒˈenderal]
sailor	**pelaut**	[pelaut]
captain	**kapten**	[kapten]
boatswain	**bosman, bosun**	[bosman], [bosun]
artilleryman	**tentara artileri**	[tentara artileri]
paratrooper	**pasukan penerjun**	[pasukan penerdʒˈun]
pilot	**pilot**	[pilot]
navigator	**navigator, penavigasi**	[navigator], [penavigasi]
mechanic	**mekanik**	[mekaniʔ]
pioneer (sapper)	**pencari ranjau**	[pentʃari randʒˈau]
parachutist	**parasutis**	[parasutis]
reconnaissance scout	**pengintai**	[peŋintaj]
sniper	**penembak jitu**	[penembaʔ dʒitu]
patrol (group)	**patroli**	[patroli]
to patrol (vt)	**berpatroli**	[bərpatroli]
sentry, guard	**pengawal**	[peŋawal]
warrior	**prajurit**	[pradʒˈurit]
patriot	**patriot**	[patriot]
hero	**pahlawan**	[pahlawan]
heroine	**pahlawan wanita**	[pahlawan wanita]
traitor	**pengkhianat**	[peŋhianat]
to betray (vt)	**mengkhianati**	[məŋhianati]
deserter	**desertir**	[desertir]
to desert (vi)	**melakukan desersi**	[melakukan desersi]
mercenary	**tentara bayaran**	[tentara bajaran]
recruit	**rekrut, calon tentara**	[rekrut], [tʃalon tentara]
volunteer	**sukarelawan**	[sukarelawan]
dead (n)	**korban meninggal**	[korban meniŋgal]
wounded (n)	**korban luka**	[korban luka]
prisoner of war	**tawanan perang**	[tawanan peraŋ]

155. War. Military actions. Part 1

war	**perang**	[peraŋ]
to be at war	**berperang**	[bərperaŋ]

civil war	perang saudara	[pəraŋ saudara]
treacherously (adv)	secara curang	[setʃara tʃuraŋ]
declaration of war	pernyataan perang	[pərnjataʔan pəraŋ]
to declare (~ war)	menyatakan perang	[mənjatakan pəraŋ]
aggression	agresi	[agresi]
to attack (invade)	menyerang	[mənjeraŋ]

to invade (vt)	menduduki	[mənduduki]
invader	penduduk	[penduduʔ]
conqueror	penakluk	[penakluʔ]

defence	pertahanan	[pərtahanan]
to defend (a country, etc.)	mempertahankan	[mempertahankan]
to defend (against ...)	bertahan ...	[bərtahan ...]

enemy	musuh	[musuh]
foe, adversary	lawan	[lawan]
enemy (as adj)	musuh	[musuh]

| strategy | strategi | [strategi] |
| tactics | taktik | [taktiʔ] |

order	perintah	[pərintah]
command (order)	perintah	[pərintah]
to order (vt)	memerintahkan	[memerintahkan]
mission	tugas	[tugas]
secret (adj)	rahasia	[rahasia]

| battle | pertempuran | [pərtempuran] |
| combat | pertempuran | [pərtempuran] |

attack	serangan	[seraŋan]
charge (assault)	serbuan	[serbuan]
to storm (vt)	menyerbu	[mənjerbu]
siege (to be under ~)	kepungan	[kepuŋan]

| offensive (n) | serangan | [seraŋan] |
| to go on the offensive | menyerang | [mənjeraŋ] |

| retreat | pengunduran | [peŋunduran] |
| to retreat (vi) | mundur | [mundur] |

| encirclement | pengepungan | [peŋepuŋan] |
| to encircle (vt) | mengepung | [məŋepuŋ] |

bombing (by aircraft)	pengeboman	[peŋeboman]
to drop a bomb	menjatuhkan bom	[məndʒ!atuhkan bom]
to bomb (vt)	mengebom	[məŋebom]
explosion	ledakan	[ledakan]

shot	tembakan	[tembakan]
to fire (~ a shot)	melepaskan	[melepaskan]
firing (burst of ~)	penembakan	[penembakan]

| to aim (to point a weapon) | membidik | [membidiʔ] |
| to point (a gun) | mengarahkan | [məŋarahkan] |

to hit (the target)	**mengenai**	[məŋenaj]
to sink (~ a ship)	**menenggelamkan**	[mənəŋgelamkan]
hole (in a ship)	**lubang**	[lubaŋ]
to founder, to sink (vi)	**karam**	[karam]
front (war ~)	**garis depan**	[garis depan]
evacuation	**evakuasi**	[evakuasi]
to evacuate (vt)	**mengevakuasi**	[məŋevakuasi]
trench	**parit perlindungan**	[parit pərlinduŋan]
barbed wire	**kawat berduri**	[kawat bərduri]
barrier (anti tank ~)	**rintangan**	[rintaŋan]
watchtower	**menara**	[mənara]
military hospital	**rumah sakit militer**	[rumah sakit militer]
to wound (vt)	**melukai**	[melukaj]
wound	**luka**	[luka]
wounded (n)	**korban luka**	[korban luka]
to be wounded	**terluka**	[tərluka]
serious (wound)	**parah**	[parah]

156. Weapons

weapons	**senjata**	[sendʒata]
firearms	**senjata api**	[sendʒata api]
cold weapons (knives, etc.)	**sejata tajam**	[sedʒata tadʒam]
chemical weapons	**senjata kimia**	[sendʒata kimia]
nuclear (adj)	**nuklir**	[nuklir]
nuclear weapons	**senjata nuklir**	[sendʒata nuklir]
bomb	**bom**	[bom]
atomic bomb	**bom atom**	[bom atom]
pistol (gun)	**pistol**	[pistol]
rifle	**senapan**	[senapan]
submachine gun	**senapan otomatis**	[senapan otomatis]
machine gun	**senapan mesin**	[senapan mesin]
muzzle	**moncong**	[montʃoŋ]
barrel	**laras**	[laras]
calibre	**kaliber**	[kaliber]
trigger	**pelatuk**	[pelatuʔ]
sight (aiming device)	**pembidik**	[pembidiʔ]
magazine	**magasin**	[magasin]
butt (shoulder stock)	**pantat senapan**	[pantat senapan]
hand grenade	**granat tangan**	[granat taŋan]
explosive	**bahan peledak**	[bahan peledaʔ]
bullet	**peluru**	[peluru]
cartridge	**patrun**	[patrun]
charge	**isian**	[isian]

ammunition	**amunisi**	[amunisi]
bomber (aircraft)	**pesawat pengebom**	[pesawat peɲebom]
fighter	**pesawat pemburu**	[pesawat pemburu]
helicopter	**helikopter**	[helikopter]
anti-aircraft gun	**meriam penangkis serangan udara**	[meriam penaŋkis seraɲan udara]
tank	**tank**	[tanʔ]
tank gun	**meriam tank**	[meriam tanʔ]
artillery	**artileri**	[artileri]
gun (cannon, howitzer)	**meriam**	[meriam]
to lay (a gun)	**mengarahkan**	[məŋarahkan]
shell (projectile)	**peluru**	[peluru]
mortar bomb	**peluru mortir**	[peluru mortir]
mortar	**mortir**	[mortir]
splinter (shell fragment)	**serpihan**	[serpihan]
submarine	**kapal selam**	[kapal selam]
torpedo	**torpedo**	[torpedo]
missile	**rudal**	[rudal]
to load (gun)	**mengisi**	[məɲisi]
to shoot (vi)	**menembak**	[mənembaʔ]
to point at (the cannon)	**membidik**	[membidiʔ]
bayonet	**bayonet**	[bajonet]
rapier	**pedang rapier**	[pedaŋ rapier]
sabre (e.g. cavalry ~)	**pedang saber**	[pedaŋ saber]
spear (weapon)	**lembing**	[lembiŋ]
bow	**busur panah**	[busur panah]
arrow	**anak panah**	[anaʔ panah]
musket	**senapan lantak**	[senapan lantaʔ]
crossbow	**busur silang**	[busur silaŋ]

157. Ancient people

primitive (prehistoric)	**primitif**	[primitif]
prehistoric (adj)	**prasejarah**	[prasedʒarah]
ancient (~ civilization)	**kuno**	[kuno]
Stone Age	**Zaman Batu**	[zaman batu]
Bronze Age	**Zaman Perunggu**	[zaman pəruŋgu]
Ice Age	**Zaman Es**	[zaman es]
tribe	**suku**	[suku]
cannibal	**kanibal**	[kanibal]
hunter	**pemburu**	[pemburu]
to hunt (vi, vt)	**berburu**	[bərburu]
mammoth	**mamut**	[mamut]
cave	**gua**	[gua]
fire	**api**	[api]

campfire	**api unggun**	[api uŋgun]
cave painting	**lukisan gua**	[lukisan gua]
tool (e.g. stone axe)	**alat kerja**	[alat kerdʒɪa]
spear	**tombak**	[tombaʔ]
stone axe	**kapak batu**	[kapaʼ batu]
to be at war	**berperang**	[bərperaŋ]
to domesticate (vt)	**menjinakkan**	[məndʒinaʼkan]
idol	**berhala**	[bərhala]
to worship (vt)	**memuja**	[memudʒɪa]
superstition	**takhayul**	[tahajul]
rite	**upacara**	[upatʃara]
evolution	**evolusi**	[evolusi]
development	**perkembangan**	[pərkembaŋan]
disappearance (extinction)	**kehilangan**	[kehilaŋan]
to adapt oneself	**menyesuaikan diri**	[mənjesuajkan diri]
archaeology	**arkeologi**	[arkeologi]
archaeologist	**arkeolog**	[arkeolog]
archaeological (adj)	**arkeologis**	[arkeologis]
excavation site	**situs ekskavasi**	[situs ekskavasi]
excavations	**ekskavasi**	[ekskavasi]
find (object)	**penemuan**	[penemuan]
fragment	**fragmen**	[fragmen]

158. Middle Ages

people (ethnic group)	**rakyat**	[rakjat]
peoples	**bangsa-bangsa**	[baŋsa-baŋsa]
tribe	**suku**	[suku]
tribes	**suku-suku**	[suku-suku]
barbarians	**kaum barbar**	[kaum barbar]
Gauls	**kaum Gaul**	[kaum gaul]
Goths	**kaum Goth**	[kaum got]
Slavs	**kaum Slavia**	[kaum slavia]
Vikings	**kaum Viking**	[kaum vikiŋ]
Romans	**kaum Roma**	[kaum roma]
Roman (adj)	**Romawi**	[romawi]
Byzantines	**kaum Byzantium**	[kaum bizantium]
Byzantium	**Byzantium**	[bizantium]
Byzantine (adj)	**Byzantium**	[bizantium]
emperor	**kaisar**	[kajsar]
leader, chief (tribal ~)	**pemimpin**	[pemimpin]
powerful (~ king)	**adikuasa, berkuasa**	[adikuasa], [bərkuasa]
king	**raja**	[radʒɪa]
ruler (sovereign)	**penguasa**	[peŋuasa]
knight	**ksatria**	[ksatria]

feudal lord	tuan	[tuan]
feudal (adj)	feodal	[feodal]
vassal	vasal	[vasal]

duke	duke	[duke]
earl	earl	[earl]
baron	baron	[baron]
bishop	uskup	[uskup]

armour	baju besi	[badʒiu besi]
shield	perisai	[pərisaj]
sword	pedang	[pedaŋ]
visor	visor, topeng besi	[visor], [topeŋ besi]
chainmail	baju zirah	[badʒiu zirah]
Crusade	Perang Salib	[pəraŋ salib]
crusader	kaum salib	[kaum salib]

territory	wilayah	[wilajah]
to attack (invade)	menyerang	[mənjeraŋ]
to conquer (vt)	menaklukkan	[mənaklu'kan]
to occupy (invade)	menduduki	[mənduduki]

siege (to be under ~)	kepungan	[kepuŋan]
besieged (adj)	terkepung	[tərkepuŋ]
to besiege (vt)	mengepung	[məŋepuŋ]

inquisition	inkuisisi	[inkuisisi]
inquisitor	inkuisitor	[inkuisitor]
torture	siksaan	[siksa'an]
cruel (adj)	kejam	[kedʒiam]
heretic	penganut bidah	[peŋanut bidah]
heresy	bidah	[bidah]

seafaring	pelayaran laut	[pelajaran laut]
pirate	bajak laut	[badʒia' laut]
piracy	pembajakan	[pembadʒiakan]
boarding (attack)	serangan terhadap kapal dari dekat	[seraŋan tərhadap kapal dari dekat]
loot, booty	rampasan	[rampasan]
treasure	harta karun	[harta karun]

discovery	penemuan	[penemuan]
to discover (new land, etc.)	menemukan	[mənemukan]
expedition	ekspedisi	[ekspedisi]

musketeer	musketir	[musketir]
cardinal	kardinal	[kardinal]
heraldry	heraldik	[heraldi']
heraldic (adj)	heraldik	[heraldi']

159. Leader. Chief. Authorities

| king | raja | [radʒia] |
| queen | ratu | [ratu] |

| royal (adj) | kerajaan, raja | [keradʒ¡a'an], [radʒ¡a] |
| kingdom | kerajaan | [keradʒ¡a'an] |

| prince | pangeran | [paŋeran] |
| princess | putri | [putri] |

president	presiden	[presiden]
vice-president	wakil presiden	[wakil presiden]
senator	senator	[senator]

monarch	monark	[monarʔ]
ruler (sovereign)	penguasa	[peŋuasa]
dictator	diktator	[diktator]
tyrant	tiran	[tiran]
magnate	magnat	[magnat]

director	direktur	[direktur]
chief	atasan	[atasan]
manager (director)	manajer	[manadʒ¡er]
boss	bos	[bos]
owner	pemilik	[pemiliʔ]

leader	pemimpin	[pemimpin]
head (~ of delegation)	kepala	[kepala]
authorities	pihak berwenang	[piha' bərwenaŋ]
superiors	atasan	[atasan]

governor	gabernur	[gabernur]
consul	konsul	[konsul]
diplomat	diplomat	[diplomat]
mayor	walikota	[walikota]
sheriff	sheriff	[ʃeriff]

emperor	kaisar	[kajsar]
tsar, czar	tsar, raja	[tsar], [radʒ¡a]
pharaoh	firaun	[firaun]
khan	khan	[han]

160. Breaking the law. Criminals. Part 1

bandit	bandit	[bandit]
crime	kejahatan	[kedʒ¡ahatan]
criminal (person)	penjahat	[pendʒ¡ahat]

thief	pencuri	[pentʃuri]
to steal (vi, vt)	mencuri	[məntʃuri]
stealing, theft	pencurian	[pentʃurian]

to kidnap (vt)	menculik	[məntʃuliʔ]
kidnapping	penculikan	[pentʃulikan]
kidnapper	penculik	[pentʃuliʔ]

| ransom | uang tebusan | [uaŋ tebusan] |
| to demand ransom | menuntut uang tebusan | [mənuntut uaŋ tebusan] |

to rob (vt)	merampok	[merampoʔ]
robbery	perampokan	[pərampokan]
robber	perampok	[pərampoʔ]

to extort (vt)	memeras	[memeras]
extortionist	pemeras	[pemeras]
extortion	pemerasan	[pemerasan]

to murder, to kill	membunuh	[membunuh]
murder	pembunuhan	[pembunuhan]
murderer	pembunuh	[pembunuh]

gunshot	tembakan	[tembakan]
to fire (~ a shot)	melepaskan	[melepaskan]
to shoot to death	menembak mati	[mənemba' mati]
to shoot (vi)	menembak	[mənembaʔ]
shooting	penembakan	[penembakan]

incident (fight, etc.)	insiden, kejadian	[insiden], [kedʒadian]
fight, brawl	perkelahian	[pərkelahian]
Help!	Tolong!	[toloŋ!]
victim	korban	[korban]

to damage (vt)	merusak	[merusaʔ]
damage	kerusakan	[kerusakan]
dead body, corpse	jenazah, mayat	[dʒenazah], [majat]
grave (~ crime)	berat	[berat]

to attack (vt)	menyerang	[mənjeraŋ]
to beat (to hit)	memukul	[memukul]
to beat up	memukuli	[memukuli]
to take (rob of sth)	merebut	[merebut]
to stab to death	menikam mati	[mənikam mati]

| to maim (vt) | mencederai | [mentʃederaj] |
| to wound (vt) | melukai | [melukaj] |

blackmail	pemerasan	[pemerasan]
to blackmail (vt)	memeras	[memeras]
blackmailer	pemeras	[pemeras]

| protection racket | pemerasan | [pemerasan] |
| racketeer | pemeras | [pemeras] |

| gangster | gangster, preman | [gaŋster], [preman] |
| mafia | mafia | [mafia] |

| pickpocket | pencopet | [pentʃopet] |
| burglar | perampok | [pərampoʔ] |

| smuggling | penyelundupan | [penjelundupan] |
| smuggler | penyelundup | [penjelundup] |

forgery	pemalsuan	[pemalsuan]
to forge (counterfeit)	memalsukan	[memalsukan]
fake (forged)	palsu	[palsu]

161. Breaking the law. Criminals. Part 2

rape	pemerkosaan	[pemerkosa'an]
to rape (vt)	memerkosa	[memerkosa]
rapist	pemerkosa	[pemerkosa]
maniac	maniak	[mania']

prostitute (fem.)	pelacur	[pelatʃur]
prostitution	pelacuran	[pelatʃuran]
pimp	germo	[germo]

| drug addict | pecandu narkoba | [petʃandu narkoba] |
| drug dealer | pengedar narkoba | [peŋedar narkoba] |

to blow up (bomb)	meledakkan	[meleda'kan]
explosion	ledakan	[ledakan]
to set fire	membakar	[membakar]
arsonist	pelaku pembakaran	[pelaku pembakaran]

terrorism	terorisme	[terorisme]
terrorist	teroris	[teroris]
hostage	sandera	[sandera]

to swindle (deceive)	menipu	[menipu]
swindle, deception	penipuan	[penipuan]
swindler	penipu	[penipu]

to bribe (vt)	menyuap	[menyuap]
bribery	penyuapan	[penyuapan]
bribe	uang suap, suapan	[uaŋ suap], [suapan]

poison	racun	[ratʃun]
to poison (vt)	meracuni	[meratʃuni]
to poison oneself	meracuni diri sendiri	[meratʃuni diri sendiri]

| suicide (act) | bunuh diri | [bunuh diri] |
| suicide (person) | pelaku bunuh diri | [pelaku bunuh diri] |

to threaten (vt)	mengancam	[meŋantʃam]
threat	ancaman	[antʃaman]
to make an attempt	melakukan percobaan pembunuhan	[melakukan pertʃoba'an pembunuhan]
attempt (attack)	percobaan pembunuhan	[pertʃoba'an pembunuhan]

| to steal (a car) | mencuri | [mentʃuri] |
| to hijack (a plane) | membajak | [membadʒʲa'] |

| revenge | dendam | [dendam] |
| to avenge (get revenge) | membalas dendam | [membalas dendam] |

to torture (vt)	menyiksa	[menjiksa]
torture	siksaan	[siksa'an]
to torment (vt)	menyiksa	[menjiksa]
pirate	bajak laut	[badʒʲa' laut]
hooligan	berandal	[berandal]

armed (adj)	bersenjata	[bərsendʒʲata]
violence	kekerasan	[kekerasan]
illegal (unlawful)	ilegal	[ilegal]
spying (espionage)	spionase	[spionase]
to spy (vi)	memata-matai	[memata-mataj]

162. Police. Law. Part 1

justice	keadilan	[keadilan]
court (see you in ~)	pengadilan	[peŋadilan]
judge	hakim	[hakim]
jurors	anggota juri	[aŋgota dʒʲuri]
jury trial	pengadilan juri	[peŋadilan dʒʲuri]
to judge, to try (vt)	mengadili	[məŋadili]
lawyer, barrister	advokat, pengacara	[advokat], [peɲatʃara]
defendant	terdakwa	[tərdakwa]
dock	bangku terdakwa	[baŋku tərdakwa]
charge	tuduhan	[tuduhan]
accused	terdakwa	[tərdakwa]
sentence	hukuman	[hukuman]
to sentence (vt)	menjatuhkan hukuman	[məndʒʲatuhkan hukuman]
guilty (culprit)	bersalah	[bərsalah]
to punish (vt)	menghukum	[məŋhukum]
punishment	hukuman	[hukuman]
fine (penalty)	denda	[denda]
life imprisonment	penjara seumur hidup	[pendʒʲara seumur hidup]
death penalty	hukuman mati	[hukuman mati]
electric chair	kursi listrik	[kursi listriʔ]
gallows	tiang gantungan	[tiaŋ gantuŋan]
to execute (vt)	menjalankan hukuman mati	[məndʒʲalankan hukuman mati]
execution	hukuman mati	[hukuman mati]
prison	penjara	[pendʒʲara]
cell	sel	[sel]
escort (convoy)	pengawal	[peɲawal]
prison officer	sipir, penjaga penjara	[sipir], [pendʒʲaga pendʒʲara]
prisoner	tahanan	[tahanan]
handcuffs	borgol	[borgol]
to handcuff (vt)	memborgol	[memborgol]
prison break	pelarian	[pelarian]
to break out (vi)	melarikan diri	[melarikan diri]
to disappear (vi)	menghilang	[məŋhilaŋ]

| to release (from prison) | membebaskan | [membebaskan] |
| amnesty | amnesti | [amnesti] |

police	polisi, kepolisian	[polisi], [kepolisian]
police officer	polisi	[polisi]
police station	kantor polisi	[kantor polisi]
truncheon	pentungan karet	[pentuŋan karet]
megaphone (loudhailer)	pengeras suara	[peŋeras suara]

patrol car	mobil patroli	[mobil patroli]
siren	sirene	[sirene]
to turn on the siren	membunyikan sirene	[membunjikan sirene]
siren call	suara sirene	[suara sirene]

crime scene	tempat kejadian perkara	[tempat kedʒʲadian pərkara]
witness	saksi	[saksi]
freedom	kebebasan	[kebebasan]
accomplice	kaki tangan	[kaki taŋan]
to flee (vi)	melarikan diri	[melarikan diri]
trace (to leave a ~)	jejak	[dʒʲedʒʲaʔ]

163. Police. Law. Part 2

search (investigation)	pencarian	[pentʃarian]
to look for ...	mencari ...	[məntʃari ...]
suspicion	kecurigaan	[ketʃuriga'an]
suspicious (e.g., ~ vehicle)	mencurigakan	[məntʃurigakan]
to stop (cause to halt)	menghentikan	[məŋhentikan]
to detain (keep in custody)	menahan	[mənahan]

case (lawsuit)	kasus, perkara	[kasus], [pərkara]
investigation	investigasi, penyidikan	[investigasi], [penjidikan]
detective	detektif	[detektif]
investigator	penyidik	[penjidiʔ]
hypothesis	hipotesis	[hipotesis]

motive	motif	[motif]
interrogation	interogasi	[interogasi]
to interrogate (vt)	menginterogasi	[məŋinterogasi]
to question	menanyai	[mənanjaj]
(~ neighbors, etc.)		
check (identity ~)	pemeriksaan	[pemeriksa'an]

round-up (raid)	razia	[razia]
search (~ warrant)	penggeledahan	[peŋgeledahan]
chase (pursuit)	pengejaran, perburuan	[peŋedʒʲaran], [pərburuan]
to pursue, to chase	mengejar	[məŋedʒʲar]
to track (a criminal)	melacak	[melatʃaʔ]

arrest	penahanan	[penahanan]
to arrest (sb)	menahan	[mənahan]
to catch (thief, etc.)	menangkap	[mənaŋkap]
capture	penangkapan	[penaŋkapan]
document	dokumen	[dokumen]

proof (evidence)	bukti	[bukti]
to prove (vt)	membuktikan	[membuktikan]
footprint	jejak	[dʒʲedʒʲaʔ]
fingerprints	sidik jari	[sidiʔ dʒʲari]
piece of evidence	barang bukti	[baraŋ bukti]

alibi	alibi	[alibi]
innocent (not guilty)	tidak bersalah	[tida' bərsalah]
injustice	ketidakadilan	[ketidakadilan]
unjust, unfair (adj)	tidak adil	[tida' adil]

criminal (adj)	pidana	[pidana]
to confiscate (vt)	menyita	[mənjita]
drug (illegal substance)	narkoba	[narkoba]
weapon, gun	senjata	[sendʒʲata]
to disarm (vt)	melucuti	[melutʃuti]
to order (command)	memerintahkan	[memerintahkan]
to disappear (vi)	menghilang	[mənhilaŋ]

law	hukum	[hukum]
legal, lawful (adj)	sah	[sah]
illegal, illicit (adj)	tidak sah	[tida' sah]

responsibility (blame)	tanggung jawab	[taŋguŋ dʒʲawab]
responsible (adj)	bertanggung jawab	[bərtaŋguŋ dʒʲawab]

NATURE

The Earth. Part 1

space	angkasa	[aŋkasa]
space (as adj)	angkasa	[aŋkasa]
outer space	ruang angkasa	[ruaŋ aŋkasa]
world	dunia	[dunia]
universe	jagat raya	[dʒ'agat raja]
galaxy	galaksi	[galaksi]
star	bintang	[bintaŋ]
constellation	gugusan bintang	[gugusan bintaŋ]
planet	planet	[planet]
satellite	satelit	[satelit]
meteorite	meteorit	[meteorit]
comet	komet	[komet]
asteroid	asteroid	[asteroid]
orbit	orbit	[orbit]
to revolve	berputar	[bərputar]
(~ around the Earth)		
atmosphere	atmosfer	[atmosfer]
the Sun	matahari	[matahari]
solar system	tata surya	[tata surja]
solar eclipse	gerhana matahari	[gerhana matahari]
the Earth	Bumi	[bumi]
the Moon	Bulan	[bulan]
Mars	Mars	[mars]
Venus	Venus	[venus]
Jupiter	Yupiter	[yupiter]
Saturn	Saturnus	[saturnus]
Mercury	Merkurius	[merkurius]
Uranus	Uranus	[uranus]
Neptune	Neptunus	[neptunus]
Pluto	Pluto	[pluto]
Milky Way	Bimasakti	[bimasakti]
Great Bear (Ursa Major)	Ursa Major	[ursa madʒor]
North Star	Bintang Utara	[bintaŋ utara]
Martian	makhluk Mars	[mahlu' mars]
extraterrestrial (n)	makhluk ruang angkasa	[mahlu' ruaŋ aŋkasa]

| alien | alien, makhluk asing | [alien], [mahluʔ asiŋ] |
| flying saucer | piring terbang | [piriŋ tərbaŋ] |

spaceship	kapal antariksa	[kapal antariksa]
space station	stasiun antariksa	[stasiun antariksa]
blast-off	peluncuran	[peluntʃuran]

engine	mesin	[mesin]
nozzle	nosel	[nosel]
fuel	bahan bakar	[bahan bakar]

cockpit, flight deck	kokpit	[kokpit]
aerial	antena	[antena]
porthole	jendela	[dʒ¡endela]
solar panel	sel surya	[sel surja]
spacesuit	pakaian antariksa	[pakajan antariksa]

| weightlessness | keadaan tanpa bobot | [keadaʔan tanpa bobot] |
| oxygen | oksigen | [oksigen] |

| docking (in space) | penggabungan | [peŋgabuŋan] |
| to dock (vi, vt) | bergabung | [bərgabuŋ] |

observatory	observatorium	[observatorium]
telescope	teleskop	[teleskop]
to observe (vt)	mengamati	[məŋamati]
to explore (vt)	mengeksplorasi	[məŋeksplorasi]

165. The Earth

the Earth	Bumi	[bumi]
the globe (the Earth)	bola Bumi	[bola bumi]
planet	planet	[planet]

atmosphere	atmosfer	[atmosfer]
geography	geografi	[geografi]
nature	alam	[alam]

globe (table ~)	globe	[globe]
map	peta	[peta]
atlas	atlas	[atlas]

| Europe | Eropa | [eropa] |
| Asia | Asia | [asia] |

| Africa | Afrika | [afrika] |
| Australia | Australia | [australia] |

America	Amerika	[amerika]
North America	Amerika Utara	[amerika utara]
South America	Amerika Selatan	[amerika selatan]

| Antarctica | Antartika | [antartika] |
| the Arctic | Arktika | [arktika] |

166. Cardinal directions

north	**utara**	[utara]
to the north	**ke utara**	[ke utara]
in the north	**di utara**	[di utara]
northern (adj)	**utara**	[utara]
south	**selatan**	[selatan]
to the south	**ke selatan**	[ke selatan]
in the south	**di selatan**	[di selatan]
southern (adj)	**selatan**	[selatan]
west	**barat**	[barat]
to the west	**ke barat**	[ke barat]
in the west	**di barat**	[di barat]
western (adj)	**barat**	[barat]
east	**timur**	[timur]
to the east	**ke timur**	[ke timur]
in the east	**di timur**	[di timur]
eastern (adj)	**timur**	[timur]

167. Sea. Ocean

sea	**laut**	[laut]
ocean	**samudra**	[samudra]
gulf (bay)	**teluk**	[teluʔ]
straits	**selat**	[selat]
land (solid ground)	**daratan**	[daratan]
continent (mainland)	**benua**	[benua]
island	**pulau**	[pulau]
peninsula	**semenanjung, jazirah**	[semenandʒʲuŋ], [dʒʲazirah]
archipelago	**kepulauan**	[kepulauan]
bay, cove	**teluk**	[teluʔ]
harbour	**pelabuhan**	[pelabuhan]
lagoon	**laguna**	[laguna]
cape	**tanjung**	[tandʒʲuŋ]
atoll	**pulau karang**	[pulau karaŋ]
reef	**terumbu**	[terumbu]
coral	**karang**	[karaŋ]
coral reef	**terumbu karang**	[terumbu karaŋ]
deep (adj)	**dalam**	[dalam]
depth (deep water)	**kedalaman**	[kedalaman]
abyss	**jurang**	[dʒʲuraŋ]
trench (e.g. Mariana ~)	**palung**	[paluŋ]
current (Ocean ~)	**arus**	[arus]
to surround (bathe)	**berbatasan dengan**	[berbatasan deŋan]

| shore | pantai | [pantaj] |
| coast | pantai | [pantaj] |

flow (flood tide)	air pasang	[air pasaŋ]
ebb (ebb tide)	air surut	[air surut]
shoal	beting	[betiŋ]
bottom (~ of the sea)	dasar	[dasar]

wave	gelombang	[gelombaŋ]
crest (~ of a wave)	puncak gelombang	[puntʃa' gelombaŋ]
spume (sea foam)	busa, buih	[busa], [buih]

storm (sea storm)	badai	[badaj]
hurricane	topan	[topan]
tsunami	tsunami	[tsunami]
calm (dead ~)	angin tenang	[aŋin tenaŋ]
quiet, calm (adj)	tenang	[tenaŋ]

| pole | kutub | [kutub] |
| polar (adj) | kutub | [kutub] |

latitude	lintang	[lintaŋ]
longitude	garis bujur	[garis budʒ'ur]
parallel	sejajar	[sedʒ'adʒ'ar]
equator	khatulistiwa	[hatulistiwa]

sky	langit	[laŋit]
horizon	horizon	[horizon]
air	udara	[udara]

lighthouse	mercusuar	[mertʃusuar]
to dive (vi)	menyelam	[mənjelam]
to sink (ab. boat)	karam	[karam]
treasure	harta karun	[harta karun]

168. Mountains

mountain	gunung	[gunuŋ]
mountain range	jajaran gunung	[dʒ'adʒ'aran gunuŋ]
mountain ridge	sisir gunung	[sisir gunuŋ]

summit, top	puncak	[puntʃa']
peak	puncak	[puntʃa']
foot (~ of the mountain)	kaki	[kaki]
slope (mountainside)	lereng	[lereŋ]

volcano	gunung api	[gunuŋ api]
active volcano	gunung api yang aktif	[gunuŋ api yaŋ aktif]
dormant volcano	gunung api yang tidak aktif	[gunuŋ api yaŋ tida' aktif]

eruption	erupsi, letusan	[erupsi], [letusan]
crater	kawah	[kawah]
magma	magma	[magma]
lava	lava, lahar	[lava], [lahar]

molten (~ lava)	pijar	[piʤʲar]
canyon	kanyon	[kanjon]
gorge	jurang	[ʤʲuraŋ]
crevice	celah	[ʧelah]
abyss (chasm)	jurang	[ʤʲuraŋ]

pass, col	pass, celah	[pass], [ʧelah]
plateau	plato, dataran tinggi	[plato], [dataran tiŋgi]
cliff	tebing	[tebiŋ]
hill	bukit	[bukit]

glacier	gletser	[gletser]
waterfall	air terjun	[air tərʤʲun]
geyser	geiser	[geyser]
lake	danau	[danau]

plain	dataran	[dataran]
landscape	landskap	[landskap]
echo	gema	[gema]

alpinist	pendaki gunung	[pendaki gunuŋ]
rock climber	pemanjat tebing	[pemanʤʲat tebiŋ]
to conquer (in climbing)	menaklukkan	[mənakluˀkan]
climb (an easy ~)	pendakian	[pendakian]

169. Rivers

river	sungai	[suŋaj]
spring (natural source)	mata air	[mata air]
riverbed (river channel)	badan sungai	[badan suŋaj]
basin (river valley)	basin	[basin]
to flow into …	mengalir ke …	[məŋalir ke …]

| tributary | anak sungai | [anaˀ suŋaj] |
| bank (river ~) | tebing sungai | [tebiŋ suŋaj] |

current (stream)	arus	[arus]
downstream (adv)	ke hilir	[ke hilir]
upstream (adv)	ke hulu	[ke hulu]

inundation	banjir	[banʤir]
flooding	banjir	[banʤir]
to overflow (vi)	membanjiri	[membanʤiri]
to flood (vt)	membanjiri	[membanʤiri]

| shallow (shoal) | beting | [betiŋ] |
| rapids | jeram | [ʤʲeram] |

dam	dam, bendungan	[dam], [benduŋan]
canal	kanal, terusan	[kanal], [tərusan]
reservoir (artificial lake)	waduk	[waduˀ]
sluice, lock	pintu air	[pintu air]
water body (pond, etc.)	kolam	[kolam]
swamp (marshland)	rawa	[rawa]

bog, marsh	**bencah, paya**	[bentʃah], [paja]
whirlpool	**pusaran air**	[pusaran air]
stream (brook)	**selokan**	[selokan]
drinking (ab. water)	**minum**	[minum]
fresh (~ water)	**tawar**	[tawar]
ice	**es**	[es]
to freeze over (ab. river, etc.)	**membeku**	[membeku]

170. Forest

forest, wood	**hutan**	[hutan]
forest (as adj)	**hutan**	[hutan]
thick forest	**hutan lebat**	[hutan lebat]
grove	**hutan kecil**	[hutan ketʃil]
forest clearing	**pembukaan hutan**	[pembukaʔan hutan]
thicket	**semak belukar**	[semaʔ belukar]
scrubland	**belukar**	[belukar]
footpath (troddenpath)	**jalan setapak**	[dʒʲalan setapaʔ]
gully	**parit**	[parit]
tree	**pohon**	[pohon]
leaf	**daun**	[daun]
leaves (foliage)	**daun-daunan**	[daun-daunan]
fall of leaves	**daun berguguran**	[daun berguguran]
to fall (ab. leaves)	**luruh**	[luruh]
top (of the tree)	**puncak**	[puntʃaʔ]
branch	**cabang**	[tʃabaŋ]
bough	**dahan**	[dahan]
bud (on shrub, tree)	**tunas**	[tunas]
needle (of the pine tree)	**daun jarum**	[daun dʒʲarum]
fir cone	**buah pinus**	[buah pinus]
tree hollow	**lubang pohon**	[lubaŋ pohon]
nest	**sarang**	[saraŋ]
burrow (animal hole)	**lubang**	[lubaŋ]
trunk	**batang**	[bataŋ]
root	**akar**	[akar]
bark	**kulit**	[kulit]
moss	**lumut**	[lumut]
to uproot (remove trees or tree stumps)	**mencabut**	[mentʃabut]
to chop down	**menebang**	[menebaŋ]
to deforest (vt)	**deforestasi, penggundulan hutan**	[deforestasi], [peŋgundulan hutan]
tree stump	**tunggul**	[tuŋgul]

campfire	**api unggun**	[api uŋgun]
forest fire	**kebakaran hutan**	[kebakaran hutan]
to extinguish (vt)	**memadamkan**	[memadamkan]
forest ranger	**penjaga hutan**	[pendʒḁaga hutan]
protection	**perlindungan**	[pərlinduŋan]
to protect (~ nature)	**melindungi**	[melinduŋi]
poacher	**pemburu ilegal**	[pemburu ilegal]
steel trap	**perangkap**	[pəraŋkap]
to gather, to pick (vt)	**memetik**	[memetiʔ]
to lose one's way	**tersesat**	[tərsesat]

171. Natural resources

natural resources	**sumber daya alam**	[sumber daja alam]
minerals	**bahan tambang**	[bahan tambaŋ]
deposits	**endapan**	[endapan]
field (e.g. oilfield)	**ladang**	[ladaŋ]
to mine (extract)	**menambang**	[mənambaŋ]
mining (extraction)	**pertambangan**	[pertambaŋan]
ore	**bijih**	[bidʒih]
mine (e.g. for coal)	**tambang**	[tambaŋ]
shaft (mine ~)	**sumur tambang**	[sumur tambaŋ]
miner	**penambang**	[penambaŋ]
gas (natural ~)	**gas**	[gas]
gas pipeline	**pipa saluran gas**	[pipa saluran gas]
oil (petroleum)	**petroleum, minyak**	[petroleum], [minjaʔ]
oil pipeline	**pipa saluran minyak**	[pipa saluran minjaʔ]
oil well	**sumur minyak**	[sumur minjaʔ]
derrick (tower)	**menara bor minyak**	[mənara bor minjaʔ]
tanker	**kapal tangki**	[kapal taŋki]
sand	**pasir**	[pasir]
limestone	**batu kapur**	[batu kapur]
gravel	**kerikil**	[kerikil]
peat	**gambut**	[gambut]
clay	**tanah liat**	[tanah liat]
coal	**arang**	[araŋ]
iron (ore)	**besi**	[besi]
gold	**emas**	[emas]
silver	**perak**	[peraʔ]
nickel	**nikel**	[nikel]
copper	**tembaga**	[tembaga]
zinc	**seng**	[seŋ]
manganese	**mangan**	[maŋan]
mercury	**air raksa**	[air raksa]
lead	**timbal**	[timbal]
mineral	**mineral**	[mineral]

crystal	**kristal, hablur**	[kristal], [hablur]
marble	**marmer**	[marmer]
uranium	**uranium**	[uranium]

The Earth. Part 2

172. Weather

weather	**cuaca**	[ʧuatʃa]
weather forecast	**prakiraan cuaca**	[prakira'an ʧuatʃa]
temperature	**temperatur, suhu**	[temperatur], [suhu]
thermometer	**termometer**	[tərmometər]
barometer	**barometer**	[barometer]
humid (adj)	**lembap**	[lembap]
humidity	**kelembapan**	[kelembapan]
heat (extreme ~)	**panas, gerah**	[panas], [gerah]
hot (torrid)	**panas terik**	[panas təri']
it's hot	**panas**	[panas]
it's warm	**hangat**	[haŋat]
warm (moderately hot)	**hangat**	[haŋat]
it's cold	**dingin**	[diŋin]
cold (adj)	**dingin**	[diŋin]
sun	**matahari**	[matahari]
to shine (vi)	**bersinar**	[bərsinar]
sunny (day)	**cerah**	[ʧerah]
to come up (vi)	**terbit**	[terbit]
to set (vi)	**terbenam**	[tərbenam]
cloud	**awan**	[awan]
cloudy (adj)	**berawan**	[bərawan]
rain cloud	**awan mendung**	[awan menduŋ]
somber (gloomy)	**mendung**	[menduŋ]
rain	**hujan**	[huʤian]
it's raining	**hujan turun**	[huʤian turun]
rainy (~ day, weather)	**hujan**	[huʤian]
to drizzle (vi)	**gerimis**	[gerimis]
pouring rain	**hujan lebat**	[huʤian lebat]
downpour	**hujan lebat**	[huʤian lebat]
heavy (e.g. ~ rain)	**lebat**	[lebat]
puddle	**kubangan**	[kubaŋan]
to get wet (in rain)	**kehujanan**	[kehuʤianan]
fog (mist)	**kabut**	[kabut]
foggy	**berkabut**	[bərkabut]
snow	**salju**	[salʤiu]
it's snowing	**turun salju**	[turun salʤiu]

173. Severe weather. Natural disasters

thunderstorm	hujan badai	[hudʒ'an badaj]
lightning (~ strike)	kilat	[kilat]
to flash (vi)	berkilau	[bərkilau]
thunder	petir	[petir]
to thunder (vi)	bergemuruh	[bərgemuruh]
it's thundering	bergemuruh	[bərgemuruh]
hail	hujan es	[hudʒ'an es]
it's hailing	hujan es	[hudʒ'an es]
to flood (vt)	membanjiri	[membandʒiri]
flood, inundation	banjir	[bandʒir]
earthquake	gempa bumi	[gempa bumi]
tremor, shoke	gempa	[gempa]
epicentre	episentrum	[episentrum]
eruption	erupsi, letusan	[erupsi], [letusan]
lava	lava, lahar	[lava], [lahar]
twister	puting beliung	[putiŋ beliuŋ]
tornado	tornado	[tornado]
typhoon	topan	[topan]
hurricane	topan	[topan]
storm	badai	[badaj]
tsunami	tsunami	[tsunami]
cyclone	siklon	[siklon]
bad weather	cuaca buruk	[tʃuatʃa buru']
fire (accident)	kebakaran	[kebakaran]
disaster	bencana	[bentʃana]
meteorite	meteorit	[meteorit]
avalanche	longsor	[loŋsor]
snowslide	salju longsor	[saldʒ'u loŋsor]
blizzard	badai salju	[badaj saldʒ'u]
snowstorm	badai salju	[badaj saldʒ'u]

Fauna

174. Mammals. Predators

predator	**predator, pemangsa**	[predator], [pemaŋsa]
tiger	**harimau**	[harimau]
lion	**singa**	[siŋa]
wolf	**serigala**	[serigala]
fox	**rubah**	[rubah]
jaguar	**jaguar**	[dʒʲaguar]
leopard	**leopard, macan tutul**	[leopard], [matʃan tutul]
cheetah	**cheetah**	[tʃeetah]
black panther	**harimau kumbang**	[harimau kumbaŋ]
puma	**singa gunung**	[siŋa gunuŋ]
snow leopard	**harimau bintang salju**	[harimau bintaŋ saldʒʲu]
lynx	**lynx**	[links]
coyote	**koyote**	[koyot]
jackal	**jakal**	[dʒʲakal]
hyena	**hiena**	[hiena]

175. Wild animals

animal	**binatang**	[binataŋ]
beast (animal)	**binatang buas**	[binataŋ buas]
squirrel	**bajing**	[badʒiŋ]
hedgehog	**landak susu**	[landa' susu]
hare	**terwelu**	[tərwelu]
rabbit	**kelinci**	[kelintʃi]
badger	**luak**	[lua']
raccoon	**rakun**	[rakun]
hamster	**hamster**	[hamster]
marmot	**marmut**	[marmut]
mole	**tikus mondok**	[tikus mondo']
mouse	**tikus**	[tikus]
rat	**tikus besar**	[tikus besar]
bat	**kelelawar**	[kelelawar]
ermine	**ermin**	[ermin]
sable	**sabel**	[sabel]
marten	**marten**	[marten]
weasel	**musang**	[musaŋ]
mink	**cerpelai**	[tʃerpelaj]

| beaver | beaver | [beaver] |
| otter | berang-berang | [bəraŋ-bəraŋ] |

horse	kuda	[kuda]
moose	rusa besar	[rusa besar]
deer	rusa	[rusa]
camel	unta	[unta]

bison	bison	[bison]
wisent	aurochs	[oroks]
buffalo	kerbau	[kerbau]

zebra	kuda belang	[kuda belaŋ]
antelope	antelop	[antelop]
roe deer	kijang	[kidʒʲaŋ]
fallow deer	rusa	[rusa]
chamois	chamois	[ʃemva]
wild boar	babi hutan jantan	[babi hutan dʒʲantan]

whale	ikan paus	[ikan paus]
seal	anjing laut	[andʒiŋ laut]
walrus	walrus	[walrus]
fur seal	anjing laut berbulu	[andʒiŋ laut bərbulu]
dolphin	lumba-lumba	[lumba-lumba]

bear	beruang	[bəruaŋ]
polar bear	beruang kutub	[bəruaŋ kutub]
panda	panda	[panda]

monkey	monyet	[monjet]
chimpanzee	simpanse	[simpanse]
orangutan	orang utan	[oraŋ utan]
gorilla	gorila	[gorila]
macaque	kera	[kera]
gibbon	siamang, ungka	[siamaŋ], [uŋka]

elephant	gajah	[gadʒʲah]
rhinoceros	badak	[badaʔ]
giraffe	jerapah	[dʒʲerapah]
hippopotamus	kuda nil	[kuda nil]

| kangaroo | kanguru | [kaŋuru] |
| koala (bear) | koala | [koala] |

mongoose	garangan	[garaŋan]
chinchilla	chinchilla	[tʃintʃilla]
skunk	sigung	[siguŋ]
porcupine	landak	[landaʔ]

176. Domestic animals

cat	kucing betina	[kutʃiŋ betina]
tomcat	kucing jantan	[kutʃiŋ dʒʲantan]
dog	anjing	[andʒiŋ]

horse	**kuda**	[kuda]
stallion (male horse)	**kuda jantan**	[kuda dʒ'antan]
mare	**kuda betina**	[kuda betina]
cow	**sapi**	[sapi]
bull	**sapi jantan**	[sapi dʒ'antan]
ox	**lembu jantan**	[lembu dʒ'antan]
sheep (ewe)	**domba**	[domba]
ram	**domba jantan**	[domba dʒ'antan]
goat	**kambing betina**	[kambiŋ betina]
billy goat, he-goat	**kambing jantan**	[kambiŋ dʒ'antan]
donkey	**keledai**	[keledaj]
mule	**bagal**	[bagal]
pig	**babi**	[babi]
piglet	**anak babi**	[ana' babi]
rabbit	**kelinci**	[kelintʃi]
hen (chicken)	**ayam betina**	[ajam betina]
cock	**ayam jago**	[ajam dʒ'ago]
duck	**bebek**	[bebe']
drake	**bebek jantan**	[bebe' dʒ'antan]
goose	**angsa**	[aŋsa]
tom turkey, gobbler	**kalkun jantan**	[kalkun dʒ'antan]
turkey (hen)	**kalkun betina**	[kalkun betina]
domestic animals	**binatang piaraan**	[binataŋ piara'an]
tame (e.g. ~ hamster)	**jinak**	[dʒina']
to tame (vt)	**menjinakkan**	[mandʒina'kan]
to breed (vt)	**membiakkan**	[membia'kan]
farm	**peternakan**	[peternakan]
poultry	**unggas**	[uŋgas]
cattle	**ternak**	[terna']
herd (cattle)	**kawanan**	[kawanan]
stable	**kandang kuda**	[kandaŋ kuda]
pigsty	**kandang babi**	[kandaŋ babi]
cowshed	**kandang sapi**	[kandaŋ sapi]
rabbit hutch	**sangkar kelinci**	[saŋkar kelintʃi]
hen house	**kandang ayam**	[kandaŋ ajam]

177. Dogs. Dog breeds

dog	**anjing**	[andʒiŋ]
sheepdog	**anjing gembala**	[andʒiŋ gembala]
German shepherd	**anjing gembala jerman**	[andʒiŋ gembala dʒ'erman]
poodle	**pudel**	[pudel]
dachshund	**anjing tekel**	[andʒiŋ tekel]
bulldog	**buldog**	[buldog]

boxer	**boxer**	[bokser]
mastiff	**Mastiff**	[mastiff]
Rottweiler	**Rottweiler**	[rotweyler]
Doberman	**Doberman**	[doberman]
basset	**Basset**	[basset]
bobtail	**bobtail**	[bobteyl]
Dalmatian	**Dalmatian**	[dalmatian]
cocker spaniel	**Cocker Spaniel**	[koker spaniel]
Newfoundland	**Newfoundland**	[njufaundland]
Saint Bernard	**Saint Bernard**	[sen bərnar]
husky	**Husky**	[haski]
Chow Chow	**Chow Chow**	[ʧau ʧau]
spitz	**Spitz**	[spits]
pug	**Pug**	[pag]

178. Sounds made by animals

barking (n)	**salak**	[sala']
to bark (vi)	**menyalak**	[mənjala']
to miaow (vi)	**mengeong**	[məŋeoŋ]
to purr (vi)	**mendengkur**	[məndeŋkur]
to moo (vi)	**melenguh**	[meleŋuh]
to bellow (bull)	**menguak**	[meŋua']
to growl (vi)	**menggeram**	[məŋgeram]
howl (n)	**auman**	[auman]
to howl (vi)	**mengaum**	[məŋaum]
to whine (vi)	**merengek**	[mereŋe']
to bleat (sheep)	**mengembik**	[məŋembi']
to oink, to grunt (pig)	**menguik**	[meŋui']
to squeal (vi)	**memekik**	[memeki']
to croak (vi)	**berdengkang**	[bərdeŋkaŋ]
to buzz (insect)	**mendengung**	[məndeŋuŋ]
to chirp	**mencicit**	[mənʧiʧit]
(crickets, grasshopper)		

179. Birds

bird	**burung**	[buruŋ]
pigeon	**burung dara**	[buruŋ dara]
sparrow	**burung gereja**	[buruŋ geredʒ'a]
tit (great tit)	**burung tit**	[buruŋ tit]
magpie	**burung murai**	[buruŋ muraj]
raven	**burung raven**	[buruŋ raven]
crow	**burung gagak**	[buruŋ gaga']

jackdaw	**burung gagak kecil**	[buruŋ gaga' ketʃil]
rook	**burung rook**	[buruŋ roo']
duck	**bebek**	[bebe']
goose	**angsa**	[aŋsa]
pheasant	**burung kuau**	[buruŋ kuau]
eagle	**rajawali**	[radʒ'awali]
hawk	**elang**	[elaŋ]
falcon	**alap-alap**	[alap-alap]
vulture	**hering**	[heriŋ]
condor (Andean ~)	**kondor**	[kondor]
swan	**angsa**	[aŋsa]
crane	**burung jenjang**	[buruŋ dʒ'endʒ'aŋ]
stork	**bangau**	[baŋau]
parrot	**burung nuri**	[buruŋ nuri]
hummingbird	**burung kolibri**	[buruŋ kolibri]
peacock	**burung merak**	[buruŋ mera']
ostrich	**burung unta**	[buruŋ unta]
heron	**kuntul**	[kuntul]
flamingo	**burung flamingo**	[buruŋ flamiŋo]
pelican	**pelikan**	[pelikan]
nightingale	**burung bulbul**	[buruŋ bulbul]
swallow	**burung walet**	[buruŋ walet]
thrush	**burung jalak**	[buruŋ dʒ'ala']
song thrush	**burung jalak suren**	[buruŋ dʒ'ala' suren]
blackbird	**burung jalak hitam**	[buruŋ dʒ'ala' hitam]
swift	**burung apus-apus**	[buruŋ apus-apus]
lark	**burung lark**	[buruŋ lar']
quail	**burung puyuh**	[buruŋ puyuh]
woodpecker	**burung pelatuk**	[buruŋ pelatu']
cuckoo	**burung kukuk**	[buruŋ kuku']
owl	**burung hantu**	[buruŋ hantu]
eagle owl	**burung hantu bertanduk**	[buruŋ hantu bertandu']
wood grouse	**burung murai kayu**	[buruŋ muraj kaju]
black grouse	**burung belibis hitam**	[buruŋ belibis hitam]
partridge	**ayam hutan**	[ajam hutan]
starling	**burung starling**	[buruŋ starliŋ]
canary	**burung kenari**	[buruŋ kenari]
hazel grouse	**ayam hutan hazel**	[ajam hutan hazel]
chaffinch	**burung chaffinch**	[buruŋ tʃaffintʃ]
bullfinch	**burung bullfinch**	[buruŋ bullfintʃ]
seagull	**burung camar**	[buruŋ tʃamar]
albatross	**albatros**	[albatros]
penguin	**penguin**	[peŋuin]

180. Birds. Singing and sounds

to sing (vi)	menyanyi	[mənjanji]
to call (animal, bird)	berteriak	[bərteria']
to crow (cock)	berkokok	[bərkoko']
cock-a-doodle-doo	kukuruyuk	[kukuruyu']
to cluck (hen)	berkotek	[bərkote']
to caw (crow call)	berkaok-kaok	[berkao'-kao']
to quack (duck call)	meleter	[meleter]
to cheep (vi)	berdecit	[bərdetʃit]
to chirp, to twitter	berkicau	[bərkitʃau]

181. Fish. Marine animals

bream	ikan bream	[ikan bream]
carp	ikan karper	[ikan karper]
perch	ikan tilapia	[ikan tilapia]
catfish	lais junggang	[lajs dʒiuŋgaŋ]
pike	ikan pike	[ikan paik]
salmon	salmon	[salmon]
sturgeon	ikan sturgeon	[ikan sturdʒien]
herring	ikan haring	[ikan hariŋ]
Atlantic salmon	ikan salem	[ikan salem]
mackerel	ikan kembung	[ikan kembuŋ]
flatfish	ikan sebelah	[ikan sebelah]
zander, pike perch	ikan seligi tenggeran	[ikan seligi teŋgeran]
cod	ikan kod	[ikan kod]
tuna	tuna	[tuna]
trout	ikan forel	[ikan forel]
eel	belut	[belut]
electric ray	ikan pari listrik	[ikan pari listri']
moray eel	belut moray	[belut morey]
piranha	ikan piranha	[ikan piranha]
shark	ikan hiu	[ikan hiu]
dolphin	lumba-lumba	[lumba-lumba]
whale	ikan paus	[ikan paus]
crab	kepiting	[kepitiŋ]
jellyfish	ubur-ubur	[ubur-ubur]
octopus	gurita	[gurita]
starfish	bintang laut	[bintaŋ laut]
sea urchin	landak laut	[landa' laut]
seahorse	kuda laut	[kuda laut]
oyster	tiram	[tiram]
prawn	udang	[udaŋ]

| lobster | udang karang | [udaŋ karaŋ] |
| spiny lobster | lobster berduri | [lobster bərduri] |

182. Amphibians. Reptiles

| snake | ular | [ular] |
| venomous (snake) | berbisa | [bərbisa] |

viper	ular viper	[ular viper]
cobra	kobra	[kobra]
python	ular sanca	[ular santʃa]
boa	ular boa	[ular boa]

grass snake	ular tanah	[ular tanah]
rattle snake	ular derik	[ular deriʔ]
anaconda	ular anakonda	[ular anakonda]

lizard	kadal	[kadal]
iguana	iguana	[iguana]
monitor lizard	biawak	[biawaʔ]
salamander	salamander	[salamander]
chameleon	bunglon	[buŋlon]
scorpion	kalajengking	[kaladʒʲeŋkiŋ]

turtle	kura-kura	[kura-kura]
frog	katak	[kataʔ]
toad	kodok	[kodoʔ]
crocodile	buaya	[buaja]

183. Insects

insect	serangga	[seraŋga]
butterfly	kupu-kupu	[kupu-kupu]
ant	semut	[semut]
fly	lalat	[lalat]
mosquito	nyamuk	[njamuʔ]
beetle	kumbang	[kumbaŋ]

wasp	tawon	[tawon]
bee	lebah	[lebah]
bumblebee	kumbang	[kumbaŋ]
gadfly (botfly)	lalat kerbau	[lalat kerbau]

| spider | laba-laba | [laba-laba] |
| spider's web | sarang laba-laba | [saraŋ laba-laba] |

dragonfly	capung	[tʃapuŋ]
grasshopper	belalang	[belalaŋ]
moth (night butterfly)	ngengat	[ŋeŋat]

| cockroach | kecoa | [ketʃoa] |
| tick | kutu | [kutu] |

| flea | kutu loncat | [kutu lontʃat] |
| midge | agas | [agas] |

locust	belalang	[belalaŋ]
snail	siput	[siput]
cricket	jangkrik	[dʒ'aŋkri']
firefly	kunang-kunang	[kunaŋ-kunaŋ]
ladybird	kumbang koksi	[kumbaŋ koksi]
cockchafer	kumbang Cockchafer	[kumbaŋ kokʃafer]

leech	lintah	[lintah]
caterpillar	ulat	[ulat]
earthworm	cacing	[tʃatʃiŋ]
larva	larva	[larva]

184. Animals. Body parts

beak	paruh	[paruh]
wings	sayap	[sajap]
foot (of the bird)	kaki	[kaki]
feathers (plumage)	bulu-bulu	[bulu-bulu]
feather	bulu	[bulu]
crest	jambul	[dʒ'ambul]

gills	insang	[insaŋ]
spawn	telur ikan	[telur ikan]
larva	larva	[larva]
fin	sirip	[sirip]
scales (of fish, reptile)	sisik	[sisi']

fang (canine)	taring	[tariŋ]
paw (e.g. cat's ~)	kaki	[kaki]
muzzle (snout)	moncong	[montʃoŋ]
mouth (cat's ~)	mulut	[mulut]
tail	ekor	[ekor]
whiskers	kumis	[kumis]

| hoof | tapak, kuku | [tapak], [kuku] |
| horn | tanduk | [tandu'] |

carapace	cangkang	[tʃaŋkaŋ]
shell (mollusk ~)	kerang	[keraŋ]
eggshell	kulit telur	[kulit telur]

| animal's hair (pelage) | bulu | [bulu] |
| pelt (hide) | kulit | [kulit] |

185. Animals. Habitats

habitat	habitat	[habitat]
migration	migrasi	[migrasi]
mountain	gunung	[gunuŋ]

reef	**terumbu**	[tərumbu]
cliff	**tebing**	[tebiŋ]
forest	**hutan**	[hutan]
jungle	**rimba**	[rimba]
savanna	**sabana**	[sabana]
tundra	**tundra**	[tundra]
steppe	**stepa**	[stepa]
desert	**gurun**	[gurun]
oasis	**oasis, oase**	[oasis], [oase]
sea	**laut**	[laut]
lake	**danau**	[danau]
ocean	**samudra**	[samudra]
swamp (marshland)	**rawa**	[rawa]
freshwater (adj)	**air tawar**	[air tawar]
pond	**kolam**	[kolam]
river	**sungai**	[suŋaj]
den (bear's ~)	**goa**	[goa]
nest	**sarang**	[saraŋ]
tree hollow	**lubang pohon**	[lubaŋ pohon]
burrow (animal hole)	**lubang**	[lubaŋ]
anthill	**sarang semut**	[saraŋ semut]

Flora

tree	**pohon**	[pohon]
deciduous (adj)	**daun luruh**	[daun luruh]
coniferous (adj)	**pohon jarum**	[pohon ʤarum]
evergreen (adj)	**selalu hijau**	[selalu hiʤʲau]
apple tree	**pohon apel**	[pohon apel]
pear tree	**pohon pir**	[pohon pir]
sweet cherry tree	**pohon ceri manis**	[pohon ʧeri manis]
sour cherry tree	**pohon ceri asam**	[pohon ʧeri asam]
plum tree	**pohon plum**	[pohon plum]
birch	**pohon berk**	[pohon bər']
oak	**pohon eik**	[pohon ei']
linden tree	**pohon linden**	[pohon linden]
aspen	**pohon aspen**	[pohon aspen]
maple	**pohon mapel**	[pohon mapel]
spruce	**pohon den**	[pohon den]
pine	**pohon pinus**	[pohon pinus]
larch	**pohon larch**	[pohon larʧ]
fir tree	**pohon fir**	[pohon fir]
cedar	**pohon aras**	[pohon aras]
poplar	**pohon poplar**	[pohon poplar]
rowan	**pohon rowan**	[pohon rowan]
willow	**pohon dedalu**	[pohon dedalu]
alder	**pohon alder**	[pohon alder]
beech	**pohon nothofagus**	[pohon notofagus]
elm	**pohon elm**	[pohon elm]
ash (tree)	**pohon abu**	[pohon abu]
chestnut	**kastanye**	[kastanje]
magnolia	**magnolia**	[magnolia]
palm tree	**palem**	[palem]
cypress	**pokok cipres**	[poko' sipres]
mangrove	**bakau**	[bakau]
baobab	**baobab**	[baobab]
eucalyptus	**kayu putih**	[kaju putih]
sequoia	**sequoia**	[sekuoia]

bush	**rumpun**	[rumpun]
shrub	**semak**	[sema']

| grapevine | pohon anggur | [pohon aŋgur] |
| vineyard | kebun anggur | [kebun aŋgur] |

raspberry bush	pohon frambus	[pohon frambus]
blackcurrant bush	pohon blackcurrant	[pohon bleʔkaren]
redcurrant bush	pohon redcurrant	[pohon redkaren]
gooseberry bush	pohon arbei hijau	[pohon arbei hidʒ'au]

acacia	pohon akasia	[pohon akasia]
barberry	pohon barberis	[pohon barberis]
jasmine	melati	[melati]

juniper	pohon juniper	[pohon dʒ'uniper]
rosebush	pohon mawar	[pohon mawar]
dog rose	pohon mawar liar	[pohon mawar liar]

188. Mushrooms

mushroom	jamur	[dʒ'amur]
edible mushroom	jamur makanan	[dʒ'amur makanan]
poisonous mushroom	jamur beracun	[dʒ'amur beratʃun]
cap	kepala jamur	[kepala dʒ'amur]
stipe	batang jamur	[bataŋ dʒ'amur]

cep, penny bun	jamur boletus	[dʒ'amur boletus]
orange-cap boletus	jamur topi jingga	[dʒ'amur topi dʒiŋga]
birch bolete	jamur boletus berk	[dʒ'amur boletus berʔ]
chanterelle	jamur chanterelle	[dʒ'amur tʃanterelle]
russula	jamur rusula	[dʒ'amur rusula]

morel	jamur morel	[dʒ'amur morel]
fly agaric	jamur Amanita muscaria	[dʒ'amur amanita mustʃaria]
death cap	jamur topi kematian	[dʒ'amur topi kematian]

189. Fruits. Berries

| fruit | buah | [buah] |
| fruits | buah-buahan | [buah-buahan] |

apple	apel	[apel]
pear	pir	[pir]
plum	plum	[plum]

strawberry (garden ~)	stroberi	[stroberi]
sour cherry	buah ceri asam	[buah tʃeri asam]
sweet cherry	buah ceri manis	[buah tʃeri manis]
grape	buah anggur	[buah aŋgur]

raspberry	buah frambus	[buah frambus]
blackcurrant	blackcurrant	[bleʔkaren]
redcurrant	redcurrant	[redkaren]
gooseberry	buah arbei hijau	[buah arbei hidʒ'au]

cranberry	buah kranberi	[buah kranberi]
orange	jeruk manis	[dʒⁱeru' manis]
tangerine	jeruk mandarin	[dʒⁱeru' mandarin]
pineapple	nanas	[nanas]
banana	pisang	[pisaŋ]
date	buah kurma	[buah kurma]

lemon	jeruk sitrun	[dʒⁱeru' sitrun]
apricot	aprikot	[aprikot]
peach	persik	[persi']
kiwi	kiwi	[kiwi]
grapefruit	jeruk Bali	[dʒⁱeru' bali]

berry	buah beri	[buah bəri]
berries	buah-buah beri	[buah-buah bəri]
cowberry	buah cowberry	[buah kowberi]
wild strawberry	stroberi liar	[stroberi liar]
bilberry	buah bilberi	[buah bilberi]

190. Flowers. Plants

| flower | bunga | [buŋa] |
| bouquet (of flowers) | buket | [buket] |

rose (flower)	mawar	[mawar]
tulip	tulip	[tulip]
carnation	bunga anyelir	[buŋa anjelir]
gladiolus	bunga gladiol	[buŋa gladiol]

cornflower	cornflower	[kornflawa]
harebell	bunga lonceng biru	[buŋa lontʃeŋ biru]
dandelion	dandelion	[dandelion]
camomile	bunga margrit	[buŋa margrit]

aloe	lidah buaya	[lidah buaja]
cactus	kaktus	[kaktus]
rubber plant, ficus	pohon ara	[pohon ara]

lily	bunga lili	[buŋa lili]
geranium	geranium	[geranium]
hyacinth	bunga bakung lembayung	[buŋa bakuŋ lembajuŋ]

mimosa	putri malu	[putri malu]
narcissus	bunga narsis	[buŋa narsis]
nasturtium	bunga nasturtium	[buŋa nasturtium]

orchid	anggrek	[aŋgre']
peony	bunga peoni	[buŋa peoni]
violet	bunga violet	[buŋa violet]

pansy	bunga pansy	[buŋa pansi]
forget-me-not	bunga jangan-lupakan-daku	[buŋa dʒⁱaŋan-lupakan-daku]
daisy	bunga desi	[buŋa desi]

poppy	bunga madat	[buŋa madat]
hemp	rami	[rami]
mint	mint	[min]

| lily of the valley | lili lembah | [lili lembah] |
| snowdrop | bunga tetesan salju | [buŋa tetesan saldʒʲu] |

nettle	jelatang	[dʒʲelataŋ]
sorrel	daun sorrel	[daun sorrel]
water lily	lili air	[lili air]
fern	pakis	[pakis]
lichen	lichen	[litʃen]

conservatory (greenhouse)	rumah kaca	[rumah katʃa]
lawn	halaman berumput	[halaman berumput]
flowerbed	bedeng bunga	[bedeŋ buŋa]

plant	tumbuhan	[tumbuhan]
grass	rumput	[rumput]
blade of grass	sehelai rumput	[sehelaj rumput]

leaf	daun	[daun]
petal	kelopak	[kelopaʔ]
stem	batang	[bataŋ]
tuber	ubi	[ubi]

| young plant (shoot) | tunas | [tunas] |
| thorn | duri | [duri] |

to blossom (vi)	berbunga	[berbuŋa]
to fade, to wither	layu	[laju]
smell (odour)	bau	[bau]
to cut (flowers)	memotong	[memotoŋ]
to pick (a flower)	memetik	[memetiʔ]

191. Cereals, grains

grain	biji-bijian	[bidʒi-bidʒian]
cereal crops	padi-padian	[padi-padian]
ear (of barley, etc.)	bulir	[bulir]

wheat	gandum	[gandum]
rye	gandum hitam	[gandum hitam]
oats	oat	[oat]
millet	jawawut	[dʒʲawawut]
barley	jelai	[dʒʲelaj]

maize	jagung	[dʒʲagun]
rice	beras	[beras]
buckwheat	buckwheat	[bakvit]

pea plant	kacang polong	[katʃaŋ poloŋ]
kidney bean	kacang buncis	[katʃaŋ buntʃis]
soya	kacang kedelai	[katʃaŋ kedelaj]

| lentil | **kacang lentil** | [katʃaŋ lentil] |
| beans (pulse crops) | **kacang-kacangan** | [katʃaŋ-katʃaŋan] |

REGIONAL GEOGRAPHY

192. Politics. Government. Part 1

politics	**politik**	[politi']
political (adj)	**politis**	[politis]
politician	**politisi, politikus**	[politisi], [politikus]
state (country)	**negara**	[negara]
citizen	**warganegara**	[warganegara]
citizenship	**kewarganegaraan**	[kewarganegara'an]
national emblem	**lambang negara**	[lambaŋ negara]
national anthem	**lagu kebangsaan**	[lagu kebaŋsa'an]
government	**pemerintah**	[pemerintah]
head of state	**kepala negara**	[kepala negara]
parliament	**parlemen**	[parlemen]
party	**partai**	[partaj]
capitalism	**kapitalisme**	[kapitalisme]
capitalist (adj)	**kapitalis**	[kapitalis]
socialism	**sosialisme**	[sosialisme]
socialist (adj)	**sosialis**	[sosialis]
communism	**komunisme**	[komunisme]
communist (adj)	**komunis**	[komunis]
communist (n)	**orang komunis**	[oraŋ komunis]
democracy	**demokrasi**	[demokrasi]
democrat	**demokrat**	[demokrat]
democratic (adj)	**demokratis**	[demokratis]
Democratic party	**Partai Demokrasi**	[partaj demokrasi]
liberal (n)	**orang liberal**	[oraŋ liberal]
Liberal (adj)	**liberal**	[liberal]
conservative (n)	**orang yang konservatif**	[oraŋ yaŋ konservatif]
conservative (adj)	**konservatif**	[konservatif]
republic (n)	**republik**	[republi']
republican (n)	**pendukung Partai Republik**	[pendukuŋ partaj republi']
Republican party	**Partai Republik**	[partaj republi']
elections	**pemilu**	[pemilu]
to elect (vt)	**memilih**	[memilih]
elector, voter	**pemilih**	[pemilih]
election campaign	**kampanye pemilu**	[kampane pemilu]
voting (n)	**pemungutan suara**	[pemuŋutan suara]
to vote (vi)	**memberikan suara**	[memberikan suara]

suffrage, right to vote	hak suara	[ha' suara]
candidate	kandidat, calon	[kandidat], [ʧalon]
to run for (~ President)	mencalonkan diri	[mənʧalonkan diri]
campaign	kampanye	[kampanje]

opposition (as adj)	oposisi	[oposisi]
opposition (n)	oposisi	[oposisi]

visit	kunjungan	[kundʒʲuŋan]
official visit	kunjungan resmi	[kundʒʲuŋan resmi]
international (adj)	internasional	[internasional]

negotiations	negosiasi, perundingan	[negosiasi], [pərundiŋan]
to negotiate (vi)	bernegosiasi	[bərnegosiasi]

193. Politics. Government. Part 2

society	masyarakat	[maʃarakat]
constitution	Konstitusi, Undang-Undang Dasar	[konstitusi], [undaŋ-undaŋ dasar]
power (political control)	kekuasaan	[kekuasa'an]
corruption	korupsi	[korupsi]

law (justice)	hukum	[hukum]
legal (legitimate)	sah	[sah]

justice (fairness)	keadilan	[keadilan]
just (fair)	adil	[adil]

committee	komite	[komite]
bill (draft law)	rancangan undang-undang	[ranʧaŋan undaŋ-undaŋ]
budget	anggaran belanja	[aŋgaran belandʒʲa]
policy	kebijakan	[kebidʒʲakan]
reform	reformasi	[reformasi]
radical (adj)	radikal	[radikal]

power (strength, force)	kuasa	[kuasa]
powerful (adj)	adikuasa, berkuasa	[adikuasa], [bərkuasa]
supporter	pendukung	[pendukuŋ]
influence	pengaruh	[peŋaruh]

regime (e.g. military ~)	rezim	[rezim]
conflict	konflik	[konfli']
conspiracy (plot)	komplotan	[komplotan]
provocation	provokasi	[provokasi]

to overthrow (regime, etc.)	menggulingkan	[məŋguliŋkan]
overthrow (of a government)	penggulingan	[peŋguliŋan]
revolution	revolusi	[revolusi]

coup d'état	kudeta	[kudeta]
military coup	kudeta militer	[kudeta militer]
crisis	krisis	[krisis]
economic recession	resesi ekonomi	[resesi ekonomi]

demonstrator (protester)	**pendemo**	[pendemo]
demonstration	**demonstrasi**	[demonstrasi]
martial law	**darurat militer**	[darurat militer]
military base	**pangkalan militer**	[paŋkalan militer]
stability	**stabilitas**	[stabilitas]
stable (adj)	**stabil**	[stabil]
exploitation	**eksploitasi**	[eksploitasi]
to exploit (workers)	**mengeksploitasi**	[məŋeksploitasi]
racism	**rasisme**	[rasisme]
racist	**rasis**	[rasis]
fascism	**fasisme**	[fasisme]
fascist	**fasis**	[fasis]

194. Countries. Miscellaneous

foreigner	**orang asing**	[oraŋ asiŋ]
foreign (adj)	**asing**	[asiŋ]
abroad (in a foreign country)	**di luar negeri**	[di luar negeri]
emigrant	**emigran**	[emigran]
emigration	**emigrasi**	[emigrasi]
to emigrate (vi)	**beremigrasi**	[bəremigrasi]
the West	**Barat**	[barat]
the East	**Timur**	[timur]
the Far East	**Timur Jauh**	[timur dʒʲauh]
civilization	**peradaban**	[pəradaban]
humanity (mankind)	**umat manusia**	[umat manusia]
the world (earth)	**dunia**	[dunia]
peace	**perdamaian**	[pərdamajan]
worldwide (adj)	**sedunia**	[sedunia]
homeland	**tanah air**	[tanah air]
people (population)	**rakyat**	[rakjat]
population	**populasi, penduduk**	[populasi], [penduduʔ]
people (a lot of ~)	**orang-orang**	[oraŋ-oraŋ]
nation (people)	**bangsa**	[baŋsa]
generation	**generasi**	[generasi]
territory (area)	**wilayah**	[wilajah]
region	**kawasan**	[kawasan]
state (part of a country)	**negara bagian**	[negara bagian]
tradition	**tradisi**	[tradisi]
custom (tradition)	**adat**	[adat]
ecology	**ekologi**	[ekologi]
Indian (Native American)	**orang Indian**	[oraŋ indian]
Gypsy (masc.)	**lelaki Gipsi**	[lelaki gipsi]
Gypsy (fem.)	**wanita Gipsi**	[wanita gipsi]

Gypsy (adj)	Gipsi, Rom	[gipsi], [rom]
empire	kekaisaran	[kekajsaran]
colony	koloni, negeri jajahan	[koloni], [negeri dʒʲadʒʲahan]
slavery	perbudakan	[pərbudakan]
invasion	invasi, penyerbuan	[invasi], [penerbuan]
famine	kelaparan, paceklik	[kelaparan], [patʃekliˀ]

195. Major religious groups. Confessions

| religion | agama | [agama] |
| religious (adj) | religius | [religius] |

faith, belief	keyakinan, iman	[keyakinan], [iman]
to believe (in God)	percaya	[pərtʃaja]
believer	penganut agama	[penanut agama]

| atheism | ateisme | [ateisme] |
| atheist | ateis | [ateis] |

Christianity	agama Kristen	[agama kristen]
Christian (n)	orang Kristen	[oran kristen]
Christian (adj)	Kristen	[kristen]

Catholicism	agama Katolik	[agama katoliˀ]
Catholic (n)	orang Katolik	[oran katoliˀ]
Catholic (adj)	Katolik	[katoliˀ]

Protestantism	Protestanisme	[protestanisme]
Protestant Church	Gereja Protestan	[geredʒʲa protestan]
Protestant (n)	Protestan	[protestan]

Orthodoxy	Kristen Ortodoks	[kristen ortodoks]
Orthodox Church	Gereja Kristen Ortodoks	[geredʒʲa kristen ortodoks]
Orthodox (n)	Ortodoks	[ortodoks]

Presbyterianism	Gereja Presbiterian	[geredʒʲa presbiterian]
Presbyterian Church	Gereja Presbiterian	[geredʒʲa presbiterian]
Presbyterian (n)	penganut	[penanut
	Gereja Presbiterian	geredʒʲa presbiterian]

| Lutheranism | Gereja Lutheran | [geredʒʲa luteran] |
| Lutheran (n) | pengikut Gereja Lutheran | [penikut geredʒʲa luteran] |

| Baptist Church | Gereja Baptis | [geredʒʲa baptis] |
| Baptist (n) | penganut Gereja Baptis | [penanut geredʒʲa baptis] |

Anglican Church	Gereja Anglikan	[geredʒʲa anlikan]
Anglican (n)	penganut Anglikanisme	[penanut anlikanisme]
Mormonism	Mormonisme	[mormonisme]
Mormon (n)	Mormon	[mormon]

Judaism	agama Yahudi	[agama yahudi]
Jew (n)	orang Yahudi	[oran yahudi]
Buddhism	agama Buddha	[agama budda]

Buddhist (n)	penganut Buddha	[peŋanut budda]
Hinduism	agama Hindu	[agama hindu]
Hindu (n)	penganut Hindu	[peŋanut hindu]

Islam	Islam	[islam]
Muslim (n)	Muslim	[muslim]
Muslim (adj)	Muslim	[muslim]

Shiah Islam	Syi'ah	[ʃi-a]
Shiite (n)	penganut Syi'ah	[peŋanut ʃi-a]
Sunni Islam	Sunni	[sunni]
Sunnite (n)	ahli Sunni	[ahli sunni]

196. Religions. Priests

| priest | pendeta | [pendeta] |
| the Pope | Paus | [paus] |

monk, friar	biarawan, rahib	[biarawan], [rahib]
nun	biarawati	[biarawati]
pastor	pastor	[pastor]

abbot	abbas	[abbas]
vicar (parish priest)	vikaris	[vikaris]
bishop	uskup	[uskup]
cardinal	kardinal	[kardinal]

preacher	pengkhotbah	[peŋhotbah]
preaching	khotbah	[hotbah]
parishioners	ahli paroki	[ahli paroki]

| believer | penganut agama | [peŋanut agama] |
| atheist | ateis | [ateis] |

197. Faith. Christianity. Islam

| Adam | Adam | [adam] |
| Eve | Hawa | [hawa] |

God	Tuhan	[tuhan]
the Lord	Tuhan	[tuhan]
the Almighty	Yang Maha Kuasa	[yaŋ maha kuasa]

sin	dosa	[dosa]
to sin (vi)	berdosa	[bərdosa]
sinner (masc.)	pedosa lelaki	[pedosa lelaki]
sinner (fem.)	pedosa wanita	[pedosa wanita]

hell	neraka	[neraka]
paradise	surga	[surga]
Jesus	Yesus	[yesus]
Jesus Christ	Yesus Kristus	[yesus kristus]

the Holy Spirit	Roh Kudus	[roh kudus]
the Saviour	Juru Selamat	[dʒʲuru selamat]
the Virgin Mary	Perawan Maria	[pərawan maria]

the Devil	Iblis	[iblis]
devil's (adj)	setan	[setan]
Satan	setan	[setan]
satanic (adj)	setan	[setan]

angel	malaikat	[malajkat]
guardian angel	malaikat pelindung	[malajkat pelinduŋ]
angelic (adj)	malaikat	[malajkat]

apostle	rasul	[rasul]
archangel	malaikat utama	[malajkat utama]
the Antichrist	Antikristus	[antikristus]

Church	Gereja	[geredʒʲa]
Bible	Alkitab	[alkitab]
biblical (adj)	Alkitab	[alkitab]

Old Testament	Perjanjian Lama	[pərdʒʲandʒian lama]
New Testament	Perjanjian Baru	[pərdʒʲandʒian baru]
Gospel	Injil	[indʒil]
Holy Scripture	Kitab Suci	[kitab sutʃi]
Heaven	Surga	[surga]

Commandment	Perintah Allah	[pərintah allah]
prophet	nabi	[nabi]
prophecy	ramalan	[ramalan]

Allah	Allah	[alah]
Mohammed	Muhammad	[muhammad]
the Koran	Al Quran	[al kurʔan]

mosque	masjid	[masdʒid]
mullah	mullah	[mullah]
prayer	sembahyang, doa	[səmbahjaŋ], [doa]
to pray (vi, vt)	bersembahyang, berdoa	[bərsembahjaŋ], [bərdoa]

pilgrimage	ziarah	[ziarah]
pilgrim	peziarah	[peziarah]
Mecca	Mekah	[mekah]

church	gereja	[geredʒʲa]
temple	kuil, candi	[kuil], [tʃandi]
cathedral	katedral	[katedral]
Gothic (adj)	Gotik	[gotiʔ]
synagogue	sinagoga, kanisah	[sinagoga], [kanisah]
mosque	masjid	[masdʒid]

chapel	kapel	[kapel]
abbey	keabbasan	[keabbasan]
convent	biara	[biara]
monastery	biara	[biara]
bell (church ~s)	lonceng	[lontʃeŋ]

bell tower	**menara lonceng**	[mənara lontʃeŋ]
to ring (ab. bells)	**berbunyi**	[bərbunji]
cross	**salib**	[salib]
cupola (roof)	**kubah**	[kubah]
icon	**ikon**	[ikon]
soul	**jiwa**	[dʒiwa]
fate (destiny)	**takdir**	[takdir]
evil (n)	**kejahatan**	[kedʒʲahatan]
good (n)	**kebaikan**	[kebajkan]
vampire	**vampir**	[vampir]
witch (evil ~)	**tukang sihir**	[tukaŋ sihir]
demon	**iblis**	[iblis]
spirit	**roh**	[roh]
redemption (giving us ~)	**penebusan**	[penebusan]
to redeem (vt)	**menebus**	[mənebus]
church service	**misa**	[misa]
to say mass	**menyelenggarakan misa**	[mənjeleŋgarakan misa]
confession	**pengakuan dosa**	[peŋakuan dosa]
to confess (vi)	**mengaku dosa**	[məŋaku dosa]
saint (n)	**santo**	[santo]
sacred (holy)	**suci, kudus**	[sutʃi], [kudus]
holy water	**air suci**	[air sutʃi]
ritual (n)	**ritus**	[ritus]
ritual (adj)	**ritual**	[ritual]
sacrifice	**pengorbangan**	[peŋorbaŋan]
superstition	**takhayul**	[tahajul]
superstitious (adj)	**bertakhayul**	[bertahajul]
afterlife	**akhirat**	[ahirat]
eternal life	**hidup abadi**	[hidup abadi]

MISCELLANEOUS

background (green ~)	**latar belakang**	[latar belakaŋ]
balance (of the situation)	**keseimbangan**	[keseimbaŋan]
barrier (obstacle)	**rintangan**	[rintaŋan]
base (basis)	**basis, dasar**	[basis], [dasar]
beginning	**permulaan**	[pərmula'an]
category	**kategori**	[kategori]
cause (reason)	**sebab**	[sebab]
choice	**pilihan**	[pilihan]
coincidence	**kebetulan**	[kebetulan]
comfortable (~ chair)	**nyaman**	[njaman]
comparison	**perbandingan**	[pərbandiŋan]
compensation	**kompensasi, ganti rugi**	[kompensasi], [ganti rugi]
degree (extent, amount)	**tingkat**	[tiŋkat]
development	**perkembangan**	[pərkembaŋan]
difference	**perbedaan**	[pərbeda'an]
effect (e.g. of drugs)	**efek, pengaruh**	[efek], [peŋaruh]
effort (exertion)	**usaha**	[usaha]
element	**unsur**	[unsur]
end (finish)	**akhir**	[ahir]
example (illustration)	**contoh**	[tʃontoh]
fact	**fakta**	[fakta]
frequent (adj)	**kerap, sering**	[kerap], [seriŋ]
growth (development)	**pertumbuhan**	[pərtumbuhan]
help	**bantuan**	[bantuan]
ideal	**ideal**	[ideal]
kind (sort, type)	**jenis**	[dʒ'enis]
labyrinth	**labirin**	[labirin]
mistake, error	**kesalahan**	[kesalahan]
moment	**saat, waktu**	[sa'at], [waktu]
object (thing)	**objek**	[obdʒ'e']
obstacle	**rintangan**	[rintaŋan]
original (original copy)	**orisinal, dokumen asli**	[orisinal], [dokumen asli]
part (~ of sth)	**bagian**	[bagian]
particle, small part	**partikel, bagian kecil**	[partikel], [bagian ketʃil]
pause (break)	**istirahat**	[istirahat]
position	**posisi**	[posisi]
principle	**prinsip**	[prinsip]
problem	**masalah**	[masalah]
process	**proses**	[proses]

progress	kemajuan	[kemadʒʲuan]
property (quality)	sifat	[sifat]
reaction	reaksi	[reaksi]
risk	risiko	[risiko]

secret	rahasia	[rahasia]
series	rangkaian	[raŋkajan]
shape (outer form)	bentuk, rupa	[bentuk], [rupa]
situation	situasi	[situasi]
solution	solusi, penyelesaian	[solusi], [penjelesajan]

standard (adj)	standar	[standar]
standard (level of quality)	standar	[standar]
stop (pause)	perhentian	[perhentian]
style	gaya	[gaja]

system	sistem	[sistem]
table (chart)	tabel	[tabel]
tempo, rate	tempo, laju	[tempo], [ladʒʲu]
term (word, expression)	istilah	[istilah]
thing (object, item)	barang	[baraŋ]

truth (e.g. moment of ~)	kebenaran	[kebenaran]
turn (please wait your ~)	giliran	[giliran]
type (sort, kind)	jenis	[dʒʲenis]
urgent (adj)	segera	[segera]
urgently	segera	[segera]

utility (usefulness)	kegunaan	[keguna'an]
variant (alternative)	varian	[varian]
way (means, method)	cara	[tʃara]
zone	zona	[zona]